The Pastor's Guide to Leading and Living

Other books by O. S. Hawkins

When Revival Comes (with Jack R. Taylor)
After Revival Comes
Clues to a Successful Life
Where Angels Fear to Tread
Tracing the Rainbow Through the Rain
Revive Us Again
Unmasked!
Jonah: Meeting the God of the Second Chance
Getting Down to Brass Tacks
In Sheep's Clothing
Tearing Down Walls and Building Bridges
Moral Earthquakes and Secret Faults
Rebuilding: It's Never Too Late for a New Beginning
Money Talks: But What Is It Really Saying?
Shields of Brass or Shields of Gold?
Good News for Great Days
Drawing the Net
Culture Shock
High Calling, High Anxiety
The Question of Our Time
The Art of Connecting
GuideStones: Ancient Landmarks
The Pastor's Primer
Antology
More Good News for Great Days
The Joshua Code

The Pastor's Guide to Leading and Living

O. S. Hawkins

THOMAS NELSON
Since 1798

Published in Nashville, Tennessee, by Thomas Nelson. Thomas Nelson is a registered trademark of HarperCollins Christian Publishing, Inc.

Typesetting by Kevin A. Wilson, Upper Case Textual Services, Lawrence, MA.

Thomas Nelson titles may be purchased in bulk for educational, business, fundraising, or sales promotional use. For information, please e-mail SpecialMarkets@ThomasNelson.com.

ISBN 978-0-3101-4149-5 (softcover)
ISBN 978-1-4016-7570-7 (eBook)

Library of Congress Cataloging-in-Publication Data

ISBN 978-1-4016-7569-1

"My lifelong friend O. S. Hawkins provides one of the very best resources imaginable to guide pastors and church leaders towards excellence in ministry. His focus on authenticity and practical effective pastoral life and leadership will resonate with every servant of Christ. This book will be a model for Christian ministry for years to come."

Jack Graham, Pastor
Prestonwood Baptist Church

"Dr. O. S. Hawkins combines the heart of a pastor and the skill of a great leader. In this powerful new book he provides pastors with a wealth of both spiritual and practical advice. He has distilled a lifetime of pastoral experience and reflection into one unprecedented volume. Every pastor needs this book, and should keep it within a short reach."

R. Albert Mohler, Jr., President
Southern Baptist Theological Seminary
Louisville, Kentucky

To the pastor at the crossroads who labors with dedication and determination in that seemingly out of the way place where he often may wonder if he is forgotten. To you is given an incredible promise—"Shepherd the flock of God which is among you … and when the Chief Shepherd appears, you will receive the crown of glory that does not fade away" (1 Peter 5:2, 4).

Contents

Introduction

In a myriad of ways this pastor's primer you hold in your hand encapsulates more than a quarter of a century of my pastoral ministry. This journey took me from the little town of Hobart out on the southwestern plains of Oklahoma to the concrete canyons of downtown Dallas. It has been my joy and privilege to be called "pastor" to four wonderful congregations of believers across the years. While at the First Baptist Church of Hobart, Oklahoma, I learned that the pastorate is in the people business and that life is about relationships. While at the First Baptist Church of Ada, Oklahoma, those good and godly people with a rich pulpit heritage inspired me to become an expository preacher. While serving the First Baptist Church in Fort Lauderdale, Florida, for fifteen years, I had the privilege of being on the cutting edge of church growth and for that decade and a half watched God do what few local churches have been able to see and experience. Then, at the First Baptist Church in Dallas, I found anew the stewardship of pastoral authority and the respect that goes with heritage and history.

Along the way of my personal journey, I have been fortunate to have had two remarkable mentors in ministry. Dr. W. Fred Swank, my father in the ministry who led me to Christ as a seventeen-year-old young man, consistently modeled the pastor's heart before me and was my constant source of encouragement, correction, and counsel. Then, after Dr. Swank's death, Dr. W. A. Criswell "adopted" me as his own. He took me under his wing and into his heart during my days in Fort Lauderdale, and then it was my good fortune to pastor the same people he had pastored for fifty years. He was my biggest asset and greatest encouragement during my Dallas days. Both of these pastors, like righteous Abel, "though dead still speak" today through much of my own philosophy of ministry that is found in this volume.

The journey throughout this book will take us through twenty-six chapters. Each chapter contains a *PowerPoint* where we will deal with the power of the subject at hand. There is also a *PracticalPoint* where we will seek to put our hands on the handle of how "to do" ministry at the chapter's particular point of interest. This is followed by a *PressurePoint*. Here we will be cautious of various things to avoid and seek to be watchful of potential problems that could possibly arise at the point of the particular chapter's topic. Then we will come to a *PulpitPoint* where we will establish a biblical basis, using an expository sermon outline for the chapter's primary subject. Finally, each chapter will conclude with a *PersonalPoint* at which the reader will have the opportunity to make personal applications for future considerations.

As the years unfold before us, it is my prayer that some young pastor out there somewhere, perhaps going to his first pastorate, will find some nugget of truth and help from these pages in order that he might, like David, lead his people "according to the integrity of his heart, and [guide] them by the skillfulness of his hands" (Ps. 78:72).

1

The Pastor and His Purpose

PowerPoints

The pastor has been given by the Sovereign Lord the highest calling in God's economy. It is not a vocation to be chosen among several options. It is a divine, supernatural calling from the Lord. Jesus put it thus, "You did not choose Me but I chose you and appointed you that you should go and bear fruit" (John 15:16). Paul said, "I became a minister according to the gift of the grace of God given to me by the effective working of His power" (Eph. 3:7). The pastor has a special calling from God and a special gift that is given to him in order to perform the work of ministry. God's words to Jeremiah are as poignant and personal to a God-called pastor as any to be found anywhere. He said, "Before I formed you in the womb I knew you; before you were born I sanctified you; I ordained you a prophet to the nations" (Jer. 1:5). I have always considered this one of the most awesome thoughts a pastor could have. Think about it: before I was formed in my mother's womb, God knew me! But that is not all. God set me apart for a special calling and ordained me to do his will. Nothing nobler could be said of a pastor than what Paul said of David in his Pisidian

Antioch address. He said that David "served God's purpose [calling, will] in his own generation, and he fell asleep" (Acts 13:36 NIV). God's purpose is for each of us to find the will of God for our lives and then to do it.

God does not simply call the pastor into ministry; he gifts him for the tasks of the pastorate. God does not call the equipped and gifted; he equips and gifts those whom he calls. That simple statement should be a comfort and a challenge for any and all who feel God's call to ministry. We find the gift of the pastor-teacher listed among those glorious ascension gifts to the church that God bestows for the express purpose of "equipping of the saints for the work of ministry, for the edifying of the body of Christ" (Eph. 4:11–12). There is something supernatural about the God-called pastor. He has the specific spiritual gift of pastoring the church of the Lord Jesus Christ. There were days in the pastorate when the call of God upon my life was the only thing that kept me going. As soon as I sensed God's call to ministry on my life as a young college student, my pastor challenged me saying, "Son, if you can do anything else and find joy, peace, and satisfaction, go and do it. Because, if God has called you, there is no contentment to be found in doing anything else." In Psalm 16:11, it is written, "You will show me the path of life. In Your presence is fullness of joy; At Your right hand are pleasures forevermore." I have never understood how anyone could pastor any church without a definite sense of the call of God. This is our purpose, "to serve God's purpose"—his calling and his will for our lives.

Accompanying the sense of a calling to ministry is the confidence that we are "sent" by God for a special purpose. Yes, "there was a man sent from God, whose name was John" (John 1:6). Pastor, put your name there. You are the man sent from God. Think about that! God still calls and sends particular people to particular places for particular purposes. Paul asks in Romans, "How then shall they call on Him in whom they have not believed? And how shall they believe in Him of whom they have not heard? And how shall they hear without a preacher? And how shall they preach unless they are sent?" (Rom. 10:14–15). From the moment I was convinced God had called me into ministry, I have had the sense that I am a "sent man."

It was the summer before my senior year at the university where I was on track to earn my degree in business administration. I had been converted to Christ three years earlier, and as I was nearing graduation, I began to continually ask the Lord the question of Paul in Acts 9:6, "Lord, what do You want me to do?" That particular year a hurricane had swept through a part of Mexico and brought devastation to a particularly poor section of Matamoras. I journeyed there with some friends and spent time helping people rebuild their homes and lives.

God used the experience to open my heart to his calling. Riding back to Fort Worth all night on a bus, I wrestled with him and what was a growing and irresistible sense that he was calling me, setting me apart, for the work of the ministry. A few days after I returned home, a gentleman called me (totally unaware of my search for God's will in my life) and asked if I could preach on a given night at the old Union Gospel Rescue Mission downtown. I readily agreed and that simple assignment confirmed in my heart God's purpose for my life. Even as I type these words, I remember the thrill of standing behind that sacred desk in that dilapidated old room and lifting up the Lord Jesus Christ. I do not believe it was sealed in my heart, however, until I made the decision public in my own church. There was something about declaring it publicly and finding the confirmation and encouragement of my church family that sealed the decision forever in my heart. From that moment, I had the assurance that there was a man sent from God whose name was O. S.

Along the years of ministry, I have discovered a very important principle. There is a difference in an achieved ministry and a received ministry. One of the most moving passages of Scripture is found when Pastor Paul is saying a farewell to those he had pastored in Ephesus. Knowing he will see their faces no more, he says, "But none of these things move me; nor do I count my life dear to myself, so that I may finish my race with joy, and the ministry which I received from the Lord Jesus, to testify to the gospel of the grace of God" (Acts 20:24). Did you catch that phrase? "The ministry which I received from the Lord Jesus." And note the way he ends the Colossian epistle, "Take heed to the ministry which you have received in the Lord, that you may fulfill it" (Col. 4:17). Paul saw his calling as a "received ministry." We do not have a ministry. It belongs to the Lord. I must confess I cringe each and every time I hear someone talk about "my ministry." Pastor, you do not have a ministry. It is not yours. You are a steward and an ambassador. You have received a ministry from the Lord Jesus. There are stark differences between an "achieved ministry" and a "received ministry." An achieved ministry seeks the applause and the amen of men. A received ministry seeks the applause and the amen of God. An achieved ministry may succeed even though it fails. A received ministry may fail (in the eyes of men) even though it succeeds (in the eyes of God). Pastor, one of the most liberating discoveries you will ever make is to discover, or perhaps rediscover, that, like Paul, you have "received a ministry" from the Lord. The pastor's calling is to "serve God's purpose" and glorify his holy name in the process.

PracticalPoints

After I surrendered to God's call to ministry, I continued my senior year in college and finished with a bachelor of business administration degree. I then went to Southwestern Baptist Theological Seminary in Fort Worth, my hometown, to begin work on the master of divinity degree.

I had within my soul a passion and burning desire to preach, but there seemed to be no opportunities afforded me, and, what is more, I saw no possibilities on the horizon. I remember going into the student center and looking on the information board and seeing various flyers and promotional pieces of my fellow seminarians preaching at various forums such as youth revivals, youth rallies, or supply preaching assignments. And nothing came my way.

On a given day, feeling rather sorry for myself and wondering why, if God called me to preach, I was not having any opportunities, I got in my car and drove across town to talk with my pastor. W. Fred Swank was not known for his compassion on what he thought were trivial matters and could at times be rather gruff. I walked into his office and poured out my dilemma to him. Poor me! He looked up from his desk and abruptly said, "Son, you be faithful over little things and God will make you ruler over greater things. Now, go on your way and close the door when you leave." That was it! I got in my car and you can probably still see the stripes of black rubber marks in the parking lot. I was incensed at his "insensitivity." "You be faithful over little things."

I started driving down Lancaster Street repeating those words sarcastically over and over—"You be faithful over little things." I passed a nursing home I had seen a thousand times but never really saw it until that day. Without thinking, I turned into the parking lot. I went in and met the manager, and she agreed to let me start coming there on Sunday afternoons and have services for the residents. I got back in my car and drove downtown to lower Houston Street and pulled up to a rescue mission. I went in and met Brother Williams who ran it, and he agreed to let me come there on Tuesday evenings and preach to the skid row inhabitants of his mission.

That advice Dr. Swank gave me was the greatest I ever received. I can tell you that today, more than thirty-five years later, there has not been a week go by in my life when I have not had multiple opportunities to preach the unsearchable riches of Christ. Pastor, one of the most practical things we can do is to be faithful over little things. When we are, God has his own ways of enlarging our coasts and expanding our opportunities.

One of the questions that sometimes challenges us is "How can I know that God is calling me to a certain purpose or place? How can I be sure?" Apart from the supernatural phenomenon of my spirit bearing witness with his own spirit within my heart confirming my calling, there are three practical approaches to finding God's will.

The first word is *desire*. I do not believe that God will call you to any particular calling without first implanting a desire in your heart to do so. The psalmist said, "Delight yourself also in the LORD, and He shall give you the desires of your heart" (Ps. 37:4). Now, this does not mean that whatever your little heart desires, God will give you. It means that God will implant those desires in your heart to do his will. God will give you the desire. We sometimes hear someone testify that "God called me to preach, but I did not want to do it." I have difficulty with that because if God is calling us to preach, he will begin by giving us the desire to do so.

The second operative word is *opportunity*. In seeking to discover God's will, desire is not enough. It must be accompanied by an opportunity. More than one of us have had a "desire" to be pastor of such and such a church, but it was not God's will for us because the opportunity did not present itself. For example, I may have the desire to be the next Billy Graham (incidentally, I do not), but it obviously is not God's will for my life. I could go rent Cowboys Stadium in Arlington, Texas, where the Dallas Cowboys play, and maybe a few dozen of my friends would show up to hear me!

Third, in finding the will of God in ministry, if you have the desire and are afforded the opportunity, then my counsel is to keep on walking and trust God if it is not his will to shut the door. A good biblical example of this is in Acts 16 when Paul is heading out on his second missionary journey. He tried to go to Asia, but he was "forbidden by the Holy Spirit to preach the word" there. He tried to go to Bithynia, and when he put his hand on the doorknob there, "the Spirit did not permit" him to go in. Even though Paul had a desire to go to these places and preach, the opportunity was not afforded him. There was no rebuke here. He was simply on the move abiding in the truth of Isaiah 30:21, "Your ears shall hear a voice behind you, saying, 'This is the way, walk in it,' whenever you turn to the right hand or whenever you turn to the left." The only way we can hear a voice behind us is to be on the move. Finally, Paul gets to Troas. There, he receives the Macedonian call. The Bible records: "After he had seen the vision, immediately we sought to go to Macedonia, concluding that the Lord had called us" (Acts 16:10). The operative word here is *concluding*. This Greek word *symbibazō* means that it all came together. It is the word picture of a sweater being knitted that doesn't look like much until it is almost finished. It is the word picture of a jigsaw puzzle that makes little sense until a piece fits here, and another there, and then it all comes together. And so it is with the will of God. It begins with desire; then there is an opportunity; and if these come together, keep walking like Paul, trusting God, and if it is not his will to shut the door, it will all come together for you. Then you, too, can conclude that the Lord has called you to a particular place for a particular task.

Once the pastor has sensed the call of God to preach and has found his place of service, then it is essential from a practical point to understand his role as a God-called pastor. Peter's first letter, and specifically chapter 5, lays this out. Practically, in the church the pastor is called to be the spiritual leader, the servant leader, and the senior leader. Peter uses three words in 1 Peter 5 to illustrate this important role of the pastor.

The pastor's calling is to be the spiritual leader of the church. Peter refers to the pastor as the *presbyteros*, translated "elder" (1 Peter 5:1). This word generally refers to a fully mature man in the faith. This may or may not have anything to do with a pastor's age. I have known men who have been in ministry for decades who do not show maturity in the faith. And I have known young men who have exhibited extraordinary maturity in ministry. This word, *elder*, carries with it a profound respect and esteem for the high calling of the office of pastor. The pastor is the spiritual leader of the church.

Peter goes on to remind us that the pastor is the servant leader of the church. He chooses the word, which in its noun form is *poimēn*, translated "shepherd," to describe this task of the pastor (1 Peter 5:2). The shepherd is to lead, feed, protect, and serve the flock of God under his care. This concept of the servant nature of the under-shepherd is found in the word *hypēretēs*, or "under rower" in other places in Scripture. This word refers to those slaves who sat down in the belly of those great Greek ships chained to the oars and rowed through the waters of the sea. This is the spirit of the pastor. He takes his place as an under rower. He doesn't have to be on deck barking out orders for others to follow. He leads with a servant's heart.

Peter continues in revealing that not only is the pastor to be the spiritual leader and servant leader of the church but also the senior leader as well. Here he chooses the word *episkopos* to describe this task (1 Peter 5:2). We translate this word "overseer." The emphasis here is on the administrative responsibilities of the pastor. Many a pastor has been less successful because he failed to see the importance of this task in ministry. If the pastor is God-anointed, God-appointed, and God-called, then no one should know what is best for the church where he serves as the pastor. He is the one whom God has appointed to give oversight to the church of God. He is the one who will one day stand before God to give account for his faithfulness to this task.

Practically speaking, the local New Testament pastor is to be the spiritual leader, the servant leader, and the senior leader of the church, recognizing full well that there is a difference in an achieved ministry and a received ministry.

PressurePoints

The pastor should see himself as a "sent man." Perhaps one of the greatest pressure points in the pastorate comes at this point. The illustration of this truth is found in the description of the beginning of Paul's first missionary journey recorded for all posterity in Acts 13. He saw himself as a "sent man." After the church at Antioch had determined that God had set Paul and Barnabas apart from the others for this special calling, the Bible records, "Then, having fasted and prayed, and laid hands on them, they sent them away" (Acts 13:3). The very next verse records, "So, being sent out by the Holy Spirit, they went down to Seleucia, and from there sailed to Cyprus" (Acts 13:4). Note the word *sent* in both verses. This brings an obvious question. Who sent them? Who sends us? Verse 3 says the church "sent" them. Verse 4 says the Holy Spirit "sent" them. So what happens when a pastor is called to the church? Is it in the hands of the church to call him or does God call him? Herein lies the issue with the call of a pastor to the church.

When we read this verse in the language of the New Testament, it comes into clear focus and reveals one of the most beautiful truths of Scripture. There are two diametrically different words in Greek that we translate into our same English word, *sent*, in these two verses. In verse 3, when we read that the church "sent" them, we find the word *apoluō*. Every other time this word is translated in the New Testament it is translated as "to let go" or "to release." It is used in Acts 3:13 to describe a prisoner who has been let go or released from prison. The word in verse 4 where we read that the Holy Spirit "sent" them is a strong word with a strong preposition in front of it, *ekpempō*. This word means to thrust out, to push out, to send out.

So this raises the question. Who does the sending? The obvious answer is that the Holy Spirit "sends" a pastor to a church, and the church recognizes this and "releases" the pastor to do the work of the ministry. God still calls particular people to particular places for particular purposes. Problems arise when the church calls a pastor whom the Holy Spirit has not sent. This can happen when the pulpit committee does not give priority to the leading of God's Holy Spirit. There is the temptation to depend more on résumés and outward appearances than on the divine nature of the call. Other problems often arise when God "sends" his man to a particular church, but that church does not and will not "release" him to do the work of ministry as the spiritual, servant, and senior leader of the church. However, when you find a situation in which the Holy Spirit has "sent" the pastor to a particular church and the church realizes and recognizes it and "releases" the pastor to do the work of the ministry, you see the power of God displayed in and through the local congregation. Pastor, make sure you are "sent by the Holy Spirit" before assuming any pastorate.

PulpitPoints

The call of God

Acts 13:2

Recently, a leading seminary educator lamented the fact that so many applicants to a particular educational institution were simply searching for a vocation, and few were speaking of any sense of divine calling to the gospel ministry. When, as a young man, I was hearing God's call to my heart for ministry, my pastor, W. Fred Swank, said to me, "Son, if you can do anything else in life and find joy and contentment, go and do it; for if you can, you have not been called into ministry."

The apostle Paul did not see himself as someone who had chosen the ministry as a career change but as a "sent" man (Acts 13:3, 4). In Acts 13:2 there are four important elements related to the call of God upon our lives.

- **The call of God is personal.**

  The Holy Spirit said to those believers at Antioch, "separate Barnabas and Saul" for the particular task he had in mind. There were many others in the church at Antioch, but it was only Barnabas and Saul who received God's call to a specific task. He did not call Lucius or Simeon or Manaen or any of the others named in this church. The call of God is personal. He still calls particular people to particular places for particular purposes.

- **The call of God is purposeful.**

The Lord said "separate" for me Barnabas and Saul. The same Greek word is used in Galatians 1:15 when Paul says, "God, who separated me from my mother's womb and called me through his grace." God has a purpose for each of our lives. We are set apart by God and for God for that particular purpose, which no one can perform quite like we can when we are called and empowered by God's Spirit.

- **The call of God is practical.**

The Holy Spirit said that these two individuals were set apart "for the work" to which he had called them. Not only did God choose the men, he chose the work the men were to do. The ministry is work. When we are walking in the Spirit, we do not wear out the seat of our pants but the soles of our shoes. There is a practical part to the calling of God.

- **The call of God is providential.**

  Note: they were set apart for the work to which God called them. The Greek expression is in the perfect tense indicating that this was something in the mind of God completed in ages past. There is a very real sense in which churches do not call the servant of God. Résumés and recommendations do not place us in divinely appointed positions. The call of God is providential.

Some churches today seem to have forgotten that what we are about is supernatural. Some act as if the pastor is to be a hireling of the church. The God-called pastor does not work for the church. He has a higher calling. He loves the church and gives himself to the church and for the church, but he recognizes that he has a higher calling.

Yes, God still calls particular people to particular places for particular purposes. The call of God is personal, purposeful, practical, and providential.

PersonalPoints

_____

_____

_____

_____

_____

_____

_____

_____

_____

_____

_____

_____

_____

_____

_____

_____

_____

_____

_____

PersonalPoints

_____

_____

_____

_____

_____

_____

_____

_____

_____

_____

_____

_____

_____

_____

_____

_____

_____

_____

2

The Pastor and His Preaching

PowerPoints

High on the list of things that please God is the issue Paul mentions in the Corinthian letter when he says, "It pleased God by the foolishness of the message preached to save those who believe" (1 Cor. 1:21). Gospel preaching pleases God. It is the highest calling one can have. There is a dynamic that takes place in the preaching experience when God and man connect that cannot be found in any other type of oratory. Yes, pastor, the preaching of the gospel is your highest calling and most important task.

In interviews with 353 formerly unchurched people, Dr. Thom Rainer, president of LifeWay Christian Resources, indicated that in response to the question, "Did the pastor and his preaching play a part in your coming to the church?" 97 percent of the respondents answered in the affirmative. When asked, "What factors led you to choose this church?" 90 percent said, "the pastor and his preaching." While the pastor has voluminous duties and multitudinous tasks, nothing should be of higher priority than the assignment to preach the gospel and "rightly divide the word of truth" to the people God has assigned to him.

It has been my privilege as a pastor to be God's under-shepherd in four different churches across the years. In my last pastorate, it was my challenge and joy to preach each Sunday behind one of the most, if not the most, influential, twentieth-century pulpits in the Western world. For forty-seven years, the incomparable Dr. George W. Truett thundered the gospel message from that sacred desk. Then, for almost fifty years Dr. W. A. Criswell, the true prince of modern preachers, expounded "the unsearchable riches" with conviction, clarity, and compassion from the same pulpit. That pulpit, like most pulpits in Baptist life, stands in the middle of the building, on center stage, so to speak. It is there to make a statement that central to Baptist worship is the preaching of the Book of God to the people of God. One can walk into the worship center of a Baptist church in virtually any place in the world and the pulpit stands as an object lesson to signify the centrality of gospel preaching in the Baptist tradition.

Proclamation, the preaching of the gospel, should be central to Christian worship. The sermon is the central dynamic in the worship experience. It is the fulcrum upon which the entire service of worship hinges. Everything that comes before it should point to it, and everything that comes after it should issue out of it. Because of this, the pastor is the worship leader of the church. In too many places and in too many circumstances, worship is only identified with something we do before the sermon.

That is, we think the worship leader is one who leads choruses or spiritual songs. The dynamic of the worship experience is a complete package, and it is the sermon, the preaching of the gospel, that must be central to it. It is the pastor himself who sets the tone for worship. If he is aloof and unengaged, the people will not have a tendency to follow him. If he is flippant and carefree before his people, they will not take it seriously. If he is reverent and worshipful in his demeanor, the people will follow suit. This is not to say the pastor should not emit an attitude of joy and gladness before the people. The psalmist said to "serve the LORD with gladness" (Ps. 100:2), and he said, "I was glad when they said to me, 'Let us go into the house of the LORD'" (Ps. 122:1).

Preaching is the pastor's highest calling and most important task. As I type these words, I am recalling my first sermon as a young preacher. On a hot summer evening in June, I stood at the Union Gospel Mission in Fort Worth, Texas, and preached to a collection of homeless and hopeless people who gathered for worship, followed by a hot meal. The thrill in my heart, the humbleness of my calling, the dynamic I sensed as God took his word and sent it forth through my feeble and trembling mouth, the sheer rush of spiritual energy, and, yes, the nervousness of the moment have never left me. The preacher should preach every sermon as though it were his first and as if it might be his last. I have sought to bring that thought with me to each and every one of the thousands of preaching experiences I have had since that summer night.

In the front of my Bible are three verses that I have memorized and that I look at on the platform before I preach each message. One is found in Paul's final epistle in his second recorded letter to Timothy, when he says, "The Lord stood with me and strengthened me, so that the message might be preached fully through me" (2 Tim. 4:17). What a comfort it is to be assured that when I stand to preach, the Lord himself is standing with me and empowering me supernaturally to preach. Another verse I read before I preach and ask the Lord to incarnate in my preaching is his promise to Jeremiah, "I will make My words in your mouth fire, and this people wood, and it shall devour them" (Jer. 5:14). This dynamic word picture encourages me more than words can say to know that God can take the words of my mouth and set people on fire with them in such a way that the Word of God begins to consume them. Finally, I read Paul's prayer in Ephesians before every preaching opportunity. I join him in praying "that utterance might be given to me, that I may open my mouth boldly to make known the mystery of the gospel" (Eph. 6:19). In other words, that as I preach, I might exhibit freedom, fearlessness, and faithfulness.

Pastor, "preach the Word! Be ready in season and out of season. Convince, rebuke, exhort, with all longsuffering and teaching" (2 Tim. 4:2). Preaching is the passion of every God-anointed and appointed pastor. It is our high calling and great privilege.

PracticalPoints

The art of preaching has a very practical nature to it. In the context of Paul's preaching ministry, it is said that he and that band of early believers "turned the world upside down" (Acts 17:6). Perhaps nowhere do we find a better example of the practicality of preaching than with Paul in Thessalonica. When the great preacher arrived there, he "as his custom was, went in to them, and for three Sabbaths reasoned with them from the scriptures" (Acts 17:2). As Luke penned these words to describe the apostle's own practical approach to preaching, he chose the word *dialegomai*, which we translate in our English Bibles as "reasoned." This compound word is made up of a preposition meaning "through" and a verb meaning "to speak." Paul's practical approach to the preaching event was to "speak through" the Scripture. He was an expository preacher! Many preachers today reason with their hearers through popular psychology, current events, and such things as business motivational techniques. The preacher in the apostolic tradition is one who is expository, who "speaks through the Scriptures" from the pulpit. After all, it is the word of God which brings conviction.

In following this Thessalonican approach to practical preaching, Luke goes on to tell us that Paul not only "reasoned" with his hearers from the Scriptures but he was also "explaining" the word to them (Acts 17:3). The word we translate "explaining" in our English Bible is the word *dianoigō*, which comes once again from the preposition meaning "through" and a verb meaning "to open." Thus we see that for Paul, gospel preaching was not simply a speaking through the Scriptures but an "opening through" of the Scriptures in an explanatory way. This same Greek word appears other places in the Bible to describe the opening of the womb or the opening of a door. Here at Thessalonica, Paul was explaining the gospel: the death, burial, and resurrection of our Lord. In his practical approach to preaching here at Thessalonica, he had two themes—the cross and the resurrection. He was an astute theologian, but he never preached theology. He used theology to preach the Lord Jesus. It is our job as preachers to "open through the word" to our hearers.

Paul is not only practical in the way he reasons and explains the Scripture in the preaching experience, but Luke goes on to record that he did something else. He was also "demonstrating" (Acts 17:3) the Scriptures to his hearers. Luke chooses the word *paratithēmi* to illustrate this fact. This word comes from the preposition that means "beside" and the verb that means "to lie down" or "to lay." Hence the word literally means "to lie down alongside." In legal jargon, it is used to describe one who gives evidence, who "lays alongside" the facts certain evidence to support his or her claim or case. Paul is speaking to the modern pastor here. He is saying that we should not be afraid to "lay it out," to speak the truth in love even though it may seem offensive and even controversial. The preacher should "demonstrate" the gospel, lay alongside his message a life that gives evidence of the validity of what he preaches and proclaims. Paul presented the evidence in a very practical way at Thessalonica. This demands that the pastor have a systematic theology and a knowledge of Bible doctrine as well as a life that matches his lips.

The Bible records that the great apostle "went in to them ... And some of them were persuaded; and ... joined Paul and Silas" (Acts 17:2, 4). Paul was winsome and persuasive in his preaching. Our English word *joined* comes from *prosklēroō*, which literally means "to obtain an inheritance with." These Thessalonians heard Paul preach the gospel, and the result was that they "joined" him in the faith. This still happens today whenever and wherever the faithful preacher reasons, explains, and demonstrates the word to his people. It would do us all well to heed the words of Paul who said, "Imitate me, just as I also imitate Christ" (1 Cor. 11:1), especially when it comes to his model of biblical preaching.

Preaching to your people Sunday by Sunday, week by week, month by month, and year by year is the great joy and challenge of the preacher. Keeping the gospel relevant to the times and needs of the particular congregation is always before the pastor. This is why it is so imperative to know your people, their needs, their struggles, and their burdens as you preach to them week by week. The man who says he is only called to preach should not seek to call himself a pastor. The pastor is a unique person in God's economy, and therefore, knowing the needs of his particular congregation is paramount in the practical nature of his preaching. For example, below are three distinct series of messages I preached at various critical times in the life of my own congregation.

I came to a church that had just been through a very difficult time. Tension and strife were in the air. Relationships that had been decades in the making were tattered, frayed, and about to tear apart. I used that opportunity to preach through the little epistle of Philemon and applied it to personal relationships. After all, life is about relationships. There are only three in life. An *outward expression*. This is the relationship we have in the home, at the office, and in the social arena where we have contact with others in interpersonal relationships. There is an *inward expression*. This is the relationship we have with ourselves. Some call it self-worth. And then there is the *upward expression*. This is an awesome thought. This is the ability to come into a relationship with God through the Lord Jesus in such a way that we can know him in the intimacy of Father and child. And the bottom line? We will never be properly related to one another until we are properly related to ourselves. Much of what happens in our broken relationships outwardly is simply a projection of what is going on within us. Thus, the truth is we will never be properly related to ourselves until we come into relationship with God, knowing him in the free pardoning of sin and thus finding our self-worth in him. I preached several messages from Philemon, each with a different aspect of relationships. Below is an outline of the series:

- **The importance of affirmation of one another (vv. 4–7).**

  Paul begins his word to Philemon with a pat on the back. "Your love has given me great joy and encouragement because you, brother, have refreshed the hearts of the saints." Affirmation has a liberating effect on others.

- **The importance of accommodation of one another (vv. 8–11).**

  Here is what is known in the business world as the win/win relationship. Paul says Onesimus "once was unprofitable to you but now is profitable to you and to me."

- **The importance of acceptance of one another (vv. 12–16).**

  Forgiveness is the key to mending broken relationships. Two things must take place to mend relationships. One, there must be a repentant heart on the part of the offending party. And, two, there must be a receptive heart on the part of the offended party.

- **The importance of allegiance to one another (vv. 17–21).**

  Paul says, "if he [Onesimus] has wronged you … put that on my account." In other words, he is showing that he is committed in his relationship to Onesimus and to Philemon and is willing to stand by both of them.

- **The importance of accountability to one another (vv. 22–25).**

  Paul says, "Prepare a guest room for me." When he said that, Philemon knew he was coming by to check up on him and hold him accountable.

These challenges worked wonders in my church as we challenged each to affirm the other, accommodate one another, accept one another, be committed to one another, and hold one another accountable.

On another occasion, I found myself in a church in desperate need of "rebuilding." Often it is easier to grow a church from a little congregation than to grow an old congregation. In a new church, there are things that need to be done. In an older, more set-in-its-ways church, there are not only things that need to be done, but things that need to be undone as well. Sensing this, I preached a series through Nehemiah who knew something about rebuilding. I titled the series "Rebuilding: It Is Never Too Late for a New Beginning." Below were the messages in the series:

- **Rebuilders get started right (chapter 1).**

  How? You make an honest evaluation, identify the need, take personal responsibility, and move out of your comfort zones.

- **Rebuilders build a team spirit (chapter 2).**

  How? Start with your goal in mind. Seize your opportunities. Make a careful analysis of your situation. Motivate your people to get off dead center. Stay on track.

- **Rebuilders let go without letting up (chapter 3).**

  How? You delegate. Set clear objectives with specific tasks. Pick the right person for the right job. Be an example yourself. Hold your people accountable. Give a genuine pat on the back.

- **Rebuilders understand "YAC" is what really matters (chapter 4).**

  How? YAC is a football term acrostic that stands for "yards after contact." Deal with conflicts head-on. Make proper adjustments. Keep doing what is right. Rally your troops.

- **Rebuilders never cut what they can untie (chapter 5).**

  How? Conflict resolution is critical. There is a time to back off. There is a time to stand up. There is a time to give in. There is a time to reach out.

- **Rebuilders finish strong (chapter 6).**

  How? Stay off the side streets. Keep focused. Stay off the sidelines. Keep faithful.

On another occasion, I noted that my church was growing out of touch with the culture around it. Instead of engaging it, it seemed to retreat from it. I wanted to challenge them in a very practical way with the importance of confronting the culture without conforming to it or condoning it. I found in Daniel a perfect example and thus preached a series

of messages from Daniel that I titled "Culture Shock!"
The messages are below:

- **Part one: The remote control syndrome
  (chapter 1).**

  Don't give in—be resistant. Don't give up—be
  consistent. Don't give out—be persistent.

- **Part two: Real video: Back to the future
  (chapter 2).**

  God reveals the scope of human history with a
  statue. God reveals the hope of human history
  with a stone.

- **Part three: You have what you tolerate
  (chapter 3).**

  Learning to live with pressure. Learning to live
  with principle. Learning to live with perspective.
  Learning to live with protection.

- **Part four: On a search for significance
  (chapter 4).**

  The way down is up. The way up is down.

- **Part five: God and graffiti—the handwriting
  is on the wall (chapter 5).**

  God is speaking on the point of our pride;

our presumption; our promiscuity; and our perversion.

- **Part six: Integrity—don't leave home without it! (chapter 6).**

  Integrity is rooted in our private lives. It is reflected in our personal lives. It is reinforced in our professional lives. It is revealed in our public lives.

These are just a few examples of how to be practical in the preaching experience. On this issue I could write volumes. There is the practical nature of our very appearance as we stand to preach. We should stand with authority and, at the same time, stand in humbleness before the people. We should care for our physical appearance, our grooming, and our manners. Nothing about us should detract from the presentation of the gospel message. In chapter 23 we will deal with the importance of such things as our continued study, our own vocabulary, and proper grammar.

PressurePoints

Today's pastor is faced with the pressure, in the words of John Stott, of being careful not to "sacrifice revelation on the altar of relevancy." In a quest to be relevant to the culture, many subtly succumb to this pressure. There is a new trendy gospel propagated by some pastors that would not be recognized by our apostolic fathers who were stewards of the New Testament gospel. The New Testament gospel teaches self-denial. The new trendy gospel espouses self-fulfillment. The New Testament gospel is focused on Christ and his plan of redemption. The new trendy gospel is focused on man and his need for happiness in life. This new trendy gospel has a flawed anthropology. It tends to see the seeker as someone who is basically good and a friend of God but is simply turned off to the church because of antiquated methods. The pastor must resist the pressure to follow fad theologies and trendy methodologies.

One can identify four major de-emphases found in much of this new trendy approach to preaching. (1) There is often a de-emphasis on the ministry of the Holy Spirit. Marketing and motivational approaches to preaching have taken the Holy Spirit's place in some circles. (2) There is also a de-emphasis on expository preaching. Short narrative messages directed at felt needs are the call of the day with the new trendy approach to preaching. (3) There is also a blatant de-emphasis on doctrine. Some contend it should be avoided and refer to it as being divisive. Finally, (4) there is a de-emphasis on a confrontational approach to preaching. In other words, our preaching, say the new trendy advocates, should always be in first- or third-person plural and seldom, if ever, in second-person plural, much less second-person singular. The pastor must remember that apostolic preaching was empowered by the Holy Spirit, centered in the Word of God, filled with doctrinal truth, and confrontational in that it called upon people to take personal responsibility for their sin. The pastor should resist, at all costs, the pressure to sacrifice revelation on the altar of relevancy.

When dealing with the pressure points in preaching, I have always felt that "balance" was the key word. Paul instructed young Timothy, and us, saying, "All Scripture is given by inspiration of God, and is profitable for doctrine, for reproof, for correction, for instruction in righteousness, that the man of God may be complete, thoroughly equipped for every good work" (2 Tim. 3:16–17). The four characteristics should be applied to the preaching event in a balanced way. Our preaching should have in it an element of *doctrine*. That is, we should not shy away from the great and deep truths of the Bible. We often sell our people short at this point. Our preaching should also have the element of *reproof*. That is, it should reprove sin. It should also have elements of *correction* in it. The call to repentance is forgotten in so many pulpits. Finally, our preaching should *instruct in righteousness* in order to help the hearer apply to his or her life the Bible truths he or she has absorbed.

Balanced preaching provides a road map for men and women journeying through life. The doctrine of salvation found in Christ enables one to get started down that road. Along the way we may get off the path due to wrong decisions or rebellious acts of our own will. It is then that preaching serves to reprove us in our sin. However, it should never leave us in reproof. It is profitable for correction so that we will not get off on the same side street again. Finally, it is profitable for instruction in righteousness so that once on the right road and headed toward our final destination, we may be conformed to the image of Christ along the way. Effective and balanced preaching of the Bible will do all four of these things with which Paul challenges Timothy.

This particular pressure point appears when we are tempted to overemphasize one of these areas and ignore the others. For example, some preaching goes to seed on doctrine. Even though some pastors are orthodox in their belief system and doctrinally sound, they seldom reprove sin, correct false paths, or instruct in righteousness. Consequently, many of their churches are dead or dying even though they are doctrinally orthodox.

Other pastors have a tendency to go to seed on reproof. They feel their primary, God-given call is to reprove everyone in their sin with a self-righteous pointed finger of accusation. They seldom, if ever, teach Bible doctrine nor do they instruct in righteousness, and they seem puzzled as to why their churches continue to dwindle in number and influence in the community.

There are others who often go to seed on correction to the virtual exclusion of training in righteousness or

Spirit-filled living. They seem too busy themselves in their attempt to correct everyone else.

And yes, there are those pastors who have a tendency to overemphasize instruction in righteousness. They immerse themselves in contemporary worship forms to the extent that praise often takes priority over proclamation. They preach continually of the Spirit-filled life to the virtual exclusion of teaching and preaching sound doctrine and then wonder why their churches often fragment and follow every wind of doctrine that might blow through their community.

The apostolic preaching model in the New Testament was one of balance. They incorporated doctrine, reproof, correction, and instruction in righteousness into their messages and did so in a winsome, warm, and balanced manner. A careful analysis of Peter's Pentecostal sermon in Acts 2 and Paul's Pisidian Antioch message in Acts 13 reveals that they both incorporated all four of these elements into the preaching experience. In Acts 2 Peter taught doctrine. He pontificated about the doctrine of the deity of Christ. He reproved sin. Hear him preaching, "Him, being delivered by the determined purpose and foreknowledge of God, you have taken by lawless hands, have crucified, and put to death" (Acts 2:23). He corrected their false paths by calling for them to "repent" (Acts 2:38). And he instructed them in righteousness by encouraging them to be baptized, to get into God's

Word, to break bread together, and to grow in the grace and knowledge of our Lord (Acts 2:38–46). Peter was a balanced preacher. He avoided the pressure of going to seed on any one element and then using his pulpit for his personal prejudices. A careful reading of Paul's first recorded sermon will show that he, too, incorporated all four of these issues in his one message (Acts 13:13–41).

Pastor, resist the pressure and the temptation to use your pulpit in an unbalanced way. Examine your preaching. Emulate this apostolic model of a balanced pattern of proclamation. Paul continued throughout his life to emphasize the necessity of balance in these four areas. He wrote the book of Romans to emphasize the need of doctrine. He wrote 1 Corinthians to reveal the need of reproof. He wrote the Galatians epistle in an attempt to show the preachers the task of correction. He wrote Ephesians primarily to instruct in righteousness. The effective preacher today is a balanced preacher of the gospel.

The pastor has so much pressure from so many places, but the one pressure he must resist is to allow anything to take his focus off his preaching. He is to preach the whole counsel of God and to do it in a balanced way without fear or favor and without compromise or corruption. The pastor's task is not simply to preach, but to teach his people the Bible and its unsearchable riches and truths. He cannot possibly do this by topical preaching.

Biblically literate, mature believers are built through a consistent and balanced exposition of God's Word.

PulpitPoints

Turning the world upside down

Acts 17:1–16

Introduction

There is a new trendy approach to preaching that has infiltrated many pulpits. It basically is telling us that there are four things that need to be avoided if we want to be productive preachers today. This new trendy approach says to (1) avoid context. That is, avoid expositional preaching. If necessary, find a Scripture to allude to, which might substantiate your own motivational point. Next, it says, (2) avoid confessions. By this, it's meant to avoid any type of doctrinal truth. Proponents are convinced we cannot be dogmatic and that our hearers are not that interested in doctrine. Proponents also advocate the concept to (3) avoid controversy. That is, the call of the day is to be tolerant of others' views and beliefs. Finally, this new trendy approach calls us to (4) avoid confrontation. Let people be as they are remains the cry and concern.

In our text, we find Paul coming to the city of Thessalonica. We don't find him doing a survey to find out what the people want in a church and then tailoring his ministry to meet these desires. No, he doesn't market the church. He churches the market! He gives them what they need, not simply what they think they want. Note his preaching in this city of Macedonia. Paul is speaking to us today.

- **Instead of telling us to avoid context ... Paul says to be expository (v. 2).**

  He reasoned from the Scriptures. He spoke through the Scriptures to them in an expository fashion. The pastor should preach the Bible for two reasons. One, he is not smart enough to preach anything else. And, two, he is too smart to preach anything else.

- **Instead of telling us to avoid confessions ... Paul says to be explanatory (v. 3).**

  He explained the Scriptures to the Thessalonians. What was Paul explaining? Note verse 3. The death, burial, and resurrection of our Lord Jesus Christ. That is the gospel!

- **Instead of telling us to avoid controversy ... Paul says to be explicit (v. 3).**

  He was demonstrating to the Thessalonians from the Bible. Thayer says the Greek word in the text here means "to give as evidence." It is the word used of a lawyer who presents evidence to lay alongside the facts of his case. Paul was not avoiding any controversy here. He was explicit. He was demonstrating that Jesus of Nazareth is the Christ. He presented the evidence. This is the preacher's task.

- **Instead of telling us to avoid confrontation . . . Paul says to be expeditious (vv. 2, 4).**

  He "went in to them, reasoned with them . . . and a great multitude . . . joined Paul and Silas." His preaching confronted his hearers with the truth of the gospel and then persuasively called upon them to commit to the Lord Jesus Christ.

Conclusion

The preacher's job is not to market the church to a lost society by finding out what they want and giving it to them. Your job as a pastor is the same as it has always been for the preacher of the gospel. Your job is to preach in such a way that you church the market, penetrate a lost world, not with what they want but with what they need. And when we do, may it be said of you and me what was said of them so long ago that we, too, "turned our world upside down."

PersonalPoints

_____

_____

_____

_____

_____

_____

_____

_____

_____

_____

_____

_____

_____

_____

_____

_____

_____

_____

_____

PersonalPoints

_____

_____

_____

_____

_____

_____

_____

_____

_____

_____

_____

_____

_____

_____

_____

_____

_____

_____

3

The Pastor and His Preparation

PowerPoints

"Keep your mornings for God." A thousand times I heard those words ring from the lips of W. A. Criswell. This is excellent advice for any and all preachers of the gospel. Your mind is fresh and uncluttered from the busyness and bustle of phone calls, letters, visits, appointments, and other distractions. It was always my practice as a pastor to stay in my study during the morning hours, away from the telephone and other interruptions except in cases of emergency. King Zedekiah once asked the prophet and preacher Jeremiah, "Is there any word from the LORD?" (Jer. 37:17). This question should be burning in our minds as we study to bring the Word of God to our people Sunday by Sunday. It was for this important task that the ministry of the deacon was instituted. That is, so that the preacher might devote himself to "prayer and to the ministry of the word" (Acts 6:4). And, as we see in the life of Christ who so often "arose a great while before day" to pray, there is no better time to devote ourselves to "prayer and to the ministry of the word" and its preparation than in the morning hours.

As we prepare in the study, there should be three important questions in our minds. First, does what we are preparing to preach exalt the Lord Jesus Christ? It is amazing how many sermons one can hear today that never mention Jesus, much less his atonement. Second, we should ask ourselves if what we are preparing to preach will explain the text. It is equally amazing how little the text is explained and exegeted today even by those who consider themselves to be expository preachers. Finally, we should ask ourselves, as we prepare the message, if it will extend the gospel. We call ourselves preachers of the gospel and yet the gospel itself, that is, the death, burial, and resurrection of the Lord Jesus, is absent in so many sermons. If we go into our preparation with a concern to exalt the Lord Jesus, explain the text, and extend the gospel in every message, it will pilot us through our preparation.

The modern-day pastor is called upon to be so many things to so many people. He must schedule his study time, block it out, let nothing interfere with it, protect it at all costs, and make it high on his priority list of ministry functions. I always kept a study at my home, away from the office, in order to devote myself entirely to it. In this way, when you awake early in the morning, you can slip right into it. If you are up late at night, your study, your books, and your resources are always there before you. The pastor who is God-blessed and spiritually productive gives priority to his sermon preparation.

PracticalPoints

Now, to the more practical aspect of the pastor's preparation to preach. I believe the preaching experience is wrapped up in three areas: the hand, the heart, and the head. In other words, there is a very practical dimension that is often overlooked, there is a spiritual dimension that should always fuel our preparation, and there is an intellectual dimension that should always accompany such a serious assignment as delivering God's Word to his people.

To begin with, there is the element of the hand in sermon preparation. This is the work ethic within the body of Christ. I always considered my Monday evening and Saturday morning visitation time as an essential part of my sermon preparation itself and not just a part of the pastoral ministry I had received from the Lord.

I was fortunate to have a wonderful mentor in ministry. W. Fred Swank was pastor of the Sagamore Hill Baptist Church in Fort Worth for more than forty years, and he led me to Christ when I was seventeen years of age. When the Lord called me to preach, Dr. Swank instilled within me the passion to never stand and preach on Sunday without personally sharing the gospel with someone through the week. This not only brings credibility to the pulpit, but makes a tremendous difference in the preaching event itself. During my days of ministry at the First Baptist Church in Fort Lauderdale, Florida,

I led evangelism training and outreach on Monday evening. Hundreds of our people were involved in this outreach effort, and numbers of people would open their hearts to Christ every Monday evening upon hearing the gospel. Then on Saturday, our staff would go into the homes of those converted on Monday evenings and confirm those decisions and explain the necessity of baptism and church membership. On Sunday mornings, our staff would meet before each service and spread out over the auditorium as people gathered for worship. It was common that one of the staff members would come to me and say, "That man in the blue coat sitting in the middle section on the aisle made a decision for Christ this past Monday evening when Bill visited his home. I was there yesterday and explained baptism and church membership to him." After hearing this and getting his name, I would walk around to the gentleman, call him by name (he would be amazed the pastor knew his name), tell him I had heard of his decision, and give him an opportunity to confirm it to me. Then I would explain briefly to him that at the end of my message that morning, I was going to ask men and women who had made that decision this week to come forward and make a public pledge to Christ and that I would look for him to be the first one down the aisle. Each Sunday, by the time I stood in the pulpit to preach, it was not uncommon to know of several new converts who were already going to respond. Believe me, that does something for your preaching.

The hand, this practical element in preparation, plays a vital part in preparing to preach. It brings integrity to your message and a sense of credibility to your pulpit.

There is also the element of the heart in sermon preparation. The preacher's heart is an important part of his preparing to preach. As our church in Fort Lauderdale grew, I realized I needed a way to stay in touch with our people and somehow, someway, be able to feel their hearts as I prepared to preach to them week by week. I adapted a prayer ministry whereby I prayed for five families in our church each day. Two weeks before their appointed day, they would each receive a card from me letting them know I would be praying specifically for them and their family on the given date and encouraging them if they had a prayer request to confidentially return it to me. While the primary purpose of this endeavor was to pray for my people, it also served to burn into my heart the needs, struggles, burdens, and challenges of my people as I was preparing my weekly messages.

On Saturday mornings, I would gather in our worship center with those involved in our various prayer ministries to pray for the services on Sunday. We would scatter over the auditorium, kneeling at every seat to pray for the one sitting there the next day. Then, on Sunday mornings in worship, those in the prayer ministry were challenged to pick out someone in the building and pray for him or her during the message. They would often pray for the pulling down of such strongholds as pride, procrastination, and presumption. These various prayer efforts had an amazing effect on my own sermon preparation as I better understood my people and knew that those to whom I would be preaching would be saturated in prayer before and during the message.

In order to be effective, the sermon must emerge from a burning heart. Many great communicators produce little abiding fruit and deliver their messages with little or no anointing. To me, it was always as important what I was when I preached, as it was what I preached. The only way to keep a burning heart is to be like those disciples on the Emmaus Road whose "hearts burned" within them "as He spoke to us along the way." The pastor without a consistent and effective personal prayer and devotional life will not be effective in the pulpit for an extended period of time. The hand and the heart are vital elements in the pastor's preparation.

Of course, the head is essential in sermon preparation. That is the actual work of study. This is the intellectual aspect, the preparation stage of the sermon itself. The calling and vocation of the pastor is one in which study never stops. He should be constantly about the business of reading and studying. It was always my practice to reread two books each and every summer. One was *Preaching & Preachers* by David Martyn Lloyd-Jones, and the other was *The Preacher's Portrait* by John

Stott. They helped to keep me focused on my preaching task and served to remind me of the serious and high calling of being a steward of the gospel message.

For many, determining the text or what subject to preach is one of the most time-consuming and difficult tasks of preparation. For me, this has always been the easiest because I preach through books of the Bible and seek to do so in a culturally relevant way while being true to the text and applying it to present-day issues. Thus, my text, usually a paragraph or more of Scripture, is ever before me.

I begin by looking at the passage, living with it for a while, reading and rereading it sometimes hundreds of times. If it is short enough, I write it down on a note card and put it in my pocket for a couple of days. During the day, several times while waiting on a phone call, sitting in a traffic jam or in a doctor's waiting room or wherever, I will read it over and over. One of my common practices is to put an inflection on a different word each time I read it. I have found it helpful to read it and ask the following questions: Who? What? When? Where? How? When inflecting a different word and asking these questions, it is amazing how an analytical outline often begins to emerge.

Next, I do the exegesis of the text. So many sources are available today through Internet sites that even the preacher without a working knowledge of the biblical languages can do a proper exegesis including word study, parsing of verbs, and the like. It makes no sense to me that if we have the language in which the New Testament was given us, Greek, that the one assigned to deliver the Word to the people of God would not want to know it and use it.

After the above steps, an outline will generally emerge in my mind issuing out of what I have construed to be the specific object of the text and sermon. I go to all the commentaries at my disposal, all the information I may have in decades of filing in my filing system, and other resources I find through searching the Internet. I then take my computer and place an introduction, various points of the sermon, and a conclusion on my screen. Next, I take all the notes I have made and the resources I have read and begin to type them in at the appropriate points in the outline, usually in the order of explanation, illustration, and application under each point. Before the days of the computer, I would do this on legal pads. Once this process is complete, I begin to arrange the various notes I have under each point in an analytical manner. Now the sermon is complete and ready. Since my earliest days in my first pastorate, I have prepared each sermon with the intention that it might someday be in print. Now, I knew full well most of them would not, but this discipline forced me to be original, to footnote sources, and to prepare a complete manuscript. My sermon files today contain thousands of such messages that make for easy and readily supplied resources.

Once the sermon is completed, I will live with it the final two days or so before it is to be delivered. While I do not memorize it word for word, I am so familiar with it that I only take a brief outline of it into the pulpit. This is most often written in the margin of my Bible. Preaching without full notes has an extremely liberating effect on me.

Before preaching the message, I go back to my original three questions as best I can and ask myself again: Have I exalted the Lord Jesus in this exposition? Have I explained the text adequately? Have I extended the gospel? That is, is the gospel in the message at some point? Then I preach it, hopefully for God's glory and the people's good.

PressurePoints

Perhaps there is no greater pressure experienced by the pastor than the pressure to adequately prepare his sermons for the week. When in the pastorate, that cloud never left me. It hovered over my head all the time. As soon as I arrived home on Sunday from church, the next message was always before me. Only a pastor can know this pressure. It is ours to live with and deal with every week of our lives.

One of the biggest pressures the pastor faces with his preparation is his limitation of time. There are so many time constraints upon the pastor. It seems that everyone must see him, that he must be at every meeting, every event. The pastor must guard with all diligence his time for study. Schedule it. Block it out. Let nothing interfere with it. Give it priority. Plan your time. I always sought to have my outline by Tuesday, if possible, to begin to hang the meat and muscle on it by Wednesday, and to have it finished by Thursday in order to have Friday and Saturday for living with it in its completed form.

Perhaps the biggest pressure we face might be in going to seed on one of the three areas of preparation mentioned above: the hand, the heart, and the head. Some are tempted to spend all their preparation time on the hand and little on the heart or head. By that I mean they spend so much time touching people's lives, they have no time for spiritual preparation or study. Others spend all their time on the heart and sometimes little on the hand or head. In other words, they are devoted to the spiritual life but removed from people's needs and their own study. Then there are those who go to seed on the head. For these, all they want to do is study. They seldom touch their people. They may call themselves pastors, but they only want to be preachers. Those who get overbalanced with the hand lack authority because they are not in the Word. Those who become overbalanced with the heart lack authenticity if they do not know their people.

And those overbalanced with the head often lack anointing by discounting the spiritual aspects of the heart. We have all seen preachers who were theoretically and homiletically astute but who lacked power and anointing in preaching.

In our day, with the media infiltration and all the high-profiled preaching therein, there comes pressure for some preachers to produce in such a way that is beyond their calling and gifts. The pastor must resist this and avoid that pressure at all costs. Be yourself. You are unique. God has called you and gifted you for the task to which he placed you. Be honest in everything you do and do not hesitate to give credit where credit is due.

PulpitPoints

The apostolic preaching model

Acts 2:14–47

In his sermon on the day of Pentecost, the apostle Peter models the preaching experience and its preparation for all posterity. As we as pastors prepare to preach, we must ensure that the proclamation of the gospel must be:

- **Prophetic. "This is what was spoken by the prophet Joel" (v. 16).**

   Peter took his text from Joel, illustrated it with two psalms, and established a biblical basis for what was transpiring at Pentecost. The prophetic element of preaching issues from the exposition of Scripture. As the pastor prepares his messages, this should be foremost in his mind.

- **Plain. "Let this be known to you" (v. 14).**

  Peter did not try and make it difficult. He simply laid out the plain truth of Jesus' incarnation, death, and resurrection. As we prepare, this is a good word to us.

- **Positive. "This Jesus God has raised up" (v. 32).**

  Peter preached the good news. Our Lord is not dead. He is alive! The resurrection is where we should find our positive note in preaching and not in some superficial feel-good approach.

- **Personal. "You have taken [Jesus] by lawless hands" (v. 23).**

  Apostolic preaching was in the second person, and often in second-person singular. So much preaching today is in first- or third-person plural; that is, "we, they." Peter calls upon those who hear him to take personal responsibility for their actions. Keep this in mind as you prepare your sermon.

- **Penetrating.** **"Now when they heard this, they were cut to the heart"** (v. 37).

  What happened? Their hearts were cut. We have a word for that: conviction. Conviction is one of the lost words in today's Christian vocabulary.

- **Persuasive.** **"What shall we do?"** (v. 37)

  Peter's preaching caused men and women to ask how they might be saved. As we prepare to preach, we should remember preaching that is penetrating leads men and women to ask "What does this mean?" (v. 12) and then "What shall we do?" (v. 37).

- **Pointed.** **"Repent"** (v. 38).

  Peter pulled no punches. He called for his hearers to change their minds, turn from their ways, and repent. As we prepare, we should ask ourselves if this element is found in our messages.

- **Pious.** **"As many as the Lord our God will call"** (v. 39).

  By pious, I mean "God-fearing." Here is the realization that only God can do the convicting and converting. It is not by might nor power nor persuasive words of men but by his spirit.

- **Persistent. "With many other words he testified and exhorted them" (v. 40).**

  Peter gave a gospel invitation. He pleaded for souls that day. This should ever be in our thoughts as we prepare our sermons, and, like Peter, once the sermon is ended "with many other words," we should exhort our hearer to come to Christ.

- **Productive. "Then those who gladly received his word were baptized" (v. 41).**

  Peter's preaching was fruitful. God honored his preparation and message.

And the result? "Praising God and having favor with all the people. And the Lord added to the church daily those who were being saved" (Acts 2:47). May God grant us as we take seriously our high calling and the preparation of our sermons the same favor with God and man.

PersonalPoints

_____

_____

_____

_____

_____

_____

_____

_____

_____

_____

_____

_____

_____

_____

_____

_____

_____

_____

PersonalPoints

_____

_____

_____

_____

_____

_____

_____

_____

_____

_____

_____

_____

_____

_____

_____

_____

_____

_____

4

The Pastor and His Passion
PowerPoints

When we think of the word *passion*, our hearts immediately turn to the suffering of Christ during those long hours when he endured beatings and crucifixion. Earlier Jesus had said, "For the Son of Man has come to seek and to save that which was lost" (Luke 19:10). His passion paved the way for our own salvation. This daily reminder should be what kindles the fire that brings about the burning passion that should consume every pastor's heart. Two very important emphases result from the pastor and his passion: evangelism and missions.

"Preach the word ... do the work of an evangelist" (2 Tim. 4:2, 5). This admonition from the final words of Paul, the great missionary-evangelist, to Timothy, his son in the ministry (and to us, I might add), should be at the forefront of our pastoral ministry. It falls to the pastor to lead the way, not only in preaching and teaching the Word but also in doing the work of the evangelist. Paul is saying here that what the God-called evangelist does in his itinerant ministry, the pastor is to do in his pastoral ministry. That is, he is to make sure he leads his people by personal example in the areas of evangelism and missions.

This attitude of outreach that reminds the church that the church exists for those who are not here yet should permeate every aspect of ministry in the church. Too many churches today make most of their decisions on the basis of who is here now or, worse yet, who has been here for fifty years. The pastor should have such a burning passion for the lost at home and around the world that he leads his people to make their corporate church decisions on the basis of who is not here yet. This attitude is passion driven and close to the heart of Christ.

The Lord Jesus left us with a promise and a challenge when he ascended. He said, "You shall receive power when the Holy Spirit has come upon you; and you shall be witnesses to Me in Jerusalem, and in all Judea and Samaria, and to the end of the earth" (Acts 1:8). Our Lord left us with the reminder that we receive power from his Holy Spirit for a primary reason: "to be my witnesses." If you are born again, you have the living Christ residing in you. If you have Christ, you have the Holy Spirit. If you have the Holy Spirit, you have power. And if you have power, you are to be his witness. God does not empower the pastor with his calling and Spirit in order that he can become the judge of all matters in the church, or so he can take on the role of the prosecuting attorney, the defense, or the jury. He gives you his power in order for you to be his witness, to "preach the word . . . and do the work of an evangelist."

Pastor, as you extend Christ's appeal to others in public or in private, remember that we are not recruiters trying to entice or induce others to join our club. We are not salespeople trying to pressure others into buying our product. We are witnesses of Christ to his saving grace.

This passion in the pastor's heart should also serve as motivation for missionary advancement. These early believers, in one generation, took the gospel across the city, across the country, across the continent, and across the cosmos. In Christ's own words, we are to have a passion for the world and extend the gospel "in Jerusalem, all Judea and Samaria, and to the ends of the earth." It falls to the pastor, as the spiritual leader of the church, to set the example in evangelism and missions. Every church, which possibly can, should send their pastor on periodic mission trips to the far corners of the earth. It will enlarge the pastor's coast, kindle a fire in his soul, and make him a more passionate and evangelistic preacher and mission leader. Pastor, "preach the Word" and do not forget to "do the work of an evangelist."

PracticalPoints

The pastor's passion for evangelism and missions should be expressed in the way he extends the invitation for men and women to come to Christ and the way in which he is used of God to "call out the called." We shall now enlarge upon our PulpitPoint in chapter 3 as we examine Peter's Pentecostal proclamation and discover some very practical points on issuing Christ's public invitation in the local church.

The invitation to respond to Christ and his call should be prophetic. By this we mean it should be based in Scripture and issued with authority. Peter took his text from Joel 2, illustrated it with Psalms 16 and 110, and established a biblical basis for what was transpiring that day on the temple mount. Our public invitations to follow Christ should issue out of our preaching text and have a strong biblical basis.

In calling people to Christ publicly, we should also make sure the invitation is plain. Peter said, "Let me explain" (Acts 2:14 NIV). Many people in our pews who are the recipients of our appeals have had little or no church involvement for years. Yet we often speak to them in words and phrases we assume they understand. Many of us cast the net out each Sunday but never seem to draw it in because we assume our hearers understand what we are asking them to do, and they don't. Make it plain. Spell it out for them.

We should also make sure our evangelistic appeals are personal. Much of preaching today is done in first- or third-person plural. That is, "we" or "they." Not much preaching today follows the apostolic model of preaching in second-person singular—"you." At Pentecost, Peter says, "You [second-person singular] have taken by law-less hands, have crucified, and put to death" (Acts 2:23).

Peter, Paul, and these other New Testament pastor-evangelists called upon people to take personal responsibility for their lives and actions.

What was the result of this preaching that was prophetic, plain, and personal? It became penetrating. The Bible records "they were cut to the heart" (Acts 2:37). We have a word for that in our Christian jargon: conviction. It just might be one of the lost words in our modern Christian vocabulary. Conviction always precedes conversion. It is like birth. Birth pains always precede birth.

Another important element in the issuing of the evangelistic appeal is that it should be pointed. Upon falling under conviction, Peter's hearers began to ask, "What shall we do?" (Acts 2:37). Peter's response was in a word: "repent." Repentance is not heard in much of today's positive preaching. And yet it was not only the message of John the Baptist, but all the apostolic preachers and our Lord himself. The call to repentance is a call to change one's mind, which will result in a change of volition or will, which then results in a change of action.

Pastor, when you extend the appeal, make sure it is also plenary. In the corporate worship experience, there are many and varied needs to which our hearers may need to respond. Some churches lament the fact that more young people from their church are not surrendering to God's call to ministry. And yet in some of these very churches the appeal to ministry has not been heard from the pulpit in years.

Peter also models for us how our extension of the gospel invitation should be passionate. After concluding his sermon at Pentecost, the Bible records "with many other words he testified and exhorted them" to come to Christ (Acts 2:40). With many other words. He did not simply preach and then sit down piously. Out of a heart filled with passion, he pleaded for souls "with many other words." My pastor always told me that if I stood to preach and invited men and women to publicly respond to Christ without having invited men and women to privately come to Christ during the week, it would, in his words, "ring somewhat hollow."

The pastor's high calling is to "preach the word ... and do the work of the evangelist."

PressurePoints

As a pastor myself and an observer of pastors and pastorates over the years, it is my observation that the pressure points in the area of the pastor's passion come in maintaining a balanced ministry of evangelism and missions. Not all churches have 20/20 vision at this point. Some tend to be a bit nearsighted. That is, they consume their energies and efforts with their own "Jerusalem," the local church. Most of the stewardship of their time and budgets goes into the local setting only, and they seldom see past their own community to the needs of the world around them. Still others are a bit farsighted. They are so consumed with reaching the unreached people groups on the other side of the world that they seem to neglect those on their own street.

Those who heard Christ on the Mount of Olives before he ascended took the gospel of Christ to their own hometowns first. The passion of going to faraway places to be his witness should not supersede the importance of beginning at home. Nor should the passion to reach our own community supersede our call to the world. We cannot play leapfrog with the call and commission of Christ. Witnessing of him and for him begins in our own "Jerusalem" and extends to "the ends of the earth."

The challenge to reach a world is a daunting and awesome task today. But think about our spiritual and pastoral forefathers who began it all. For them, it seemed geographically impossible. Most people of their day believed the world was flat! It seemed physically impossible. There were no airplanes, printing presses, computers, televisions, nor evangelistic tracts. It seemed legally impossible. It became against the law to speak in Christ's name in many places. And it certainly seemed socially impossible. By and large, the church was made up of rejects, uneducated and virtually rejected from society's elite. But they did it! And they did it in one generation! They had passion and balance as they went about their work and witness.

Today's pastor is responsible to lead the church to have 20/20 vision when it comes to balancing the church's mission at home and around the world. As a Southern Baptist pastor for the duration of my pastoral ministry, I came to appreciate the genius of what Southern Baptists refer to as the Cooperative Program of mission support. This voluntary method of mission giving by more than forty thousand cooperating churches has fueled the greatest mission-sending force in church history and has maintained quality education in several first-class seminaries, as well as funded missions at home. It enabled me as a pastor to work with others in touching our world in a way I could never have known through my local church alone.

No discussion regarding evangelism and missions would be complete without reference to the Great Commission given us by the Lord himself. "All authority has been given to Me in heaven and on earth. Go therefore and make disciples of all the nations, baptizing them in the name of the Father and of the Son and of the Holy Spirit, teaching them to observe all things that I have commanded you; and lo, I am with you always, even to the end of the age" (Matt. 28:18–20).

Again, this Great Commission speaks to the pastor of the necessity of balance. There are three things we are to do and emphasize. We are to make disciples, mark disciples, and mature disciples. Our task is to make disciples, to lead men and women at home and around the world to a saving faith in Jesus Christ. Then we are to mark them by believer's baptism. This is vitally important or else Christ would not have put it in the middle of the Great Commission. We will deal with this in detail in chapter 11. Finally, Christ says we are to take these disciples who have been made and marked and mature them in the faith. The fulfillment of this commission is the passion and goal of every God-appointed and God-anointed pastor who truly does the work of the evangelist.

PulpitPoints

Coming to Christ

John 1:35–51

In these verses we find five different individuals who became followers of Christ. They displayed widely different temperaments. John was devoted and affectionate. Andrew was humble and practical. Peter was often impulsive, a classic type A personality. Philip was more skeptical by nature. And Nathanael was meditative and contemplative. They serve as examples to us of three ways people become followers of Christ. Some come to him through pulpit proclamation, some through private visitation, and others through personal confrontation.

- **Pulpit proclamation (vv. 35–39)**

  Andrew and John were part of John the Baptist's congregation down in the Jordan valley. They sat under his anointed preaching and it pointed them to the Lord Jesus. They saw John point to Jesus and heard him say, "Behold the Lamb of God," and they left to follow Christ themselves.

- **Private visitation (vv. 43–44)**

  No one is recorded as going to Philip. He was never in a preaching service. Nor did he ever read a gospel tract. The Lord Jesus appeared to him privately and bid him to follow. The Lord is still seeking to save the lost today. Here we see the Good Shepherd himself, going after the sheep.

- **Personal confrontation (vv. 40–42, 45–51)**

  Some are confronted with the claims of Christ by family and some by friends. Peter came to Christ due to the personal confrontation of his brother, Andrew. Andrew sought him, taught him, and brought him to Jesus (vv. 41–42). Nathanael, on the other hand, came by the personal confrontation of a friend, Philip (vv. 45–51), who was wise enough not to argue but to press the claims of Christ and say "come and see."

Yes, some come through pulpit proclamation, others through private visitation, but most through personal confrontation. Andrew found Peter. Philip found Nathanael and thus the church has continued to grow through the centuries. The most rapid and far-reaching results were achieved in this first generation without the use of television, Internet, air travel, or any of our modern conveniences. The gospel still spreads lip to lip, life to life, and person to person. Someone you know needs to know Jesus and is just waiting to be encouraged to "come and see."

PersonalPoints

PersonalPoints

_____

_____

_____

_____

_____

_____

_____

_____

_____

_____

_____

_____

_____

_____

_____

_____

_____

_____

PersonalPoints

_____

_____

_____

_____

_____

_____

_____

_____

_____

_____

_____

_____

_____

_____

_____

_____

_____

_____

_____

5

The Pastor and His Perspective

PowerPoints

One of the pastor's most important tasks lies in the realm of his perspective for his church, his God-given vision for the church to which he has been called. It falls upon the pastor to cast the vision of what God intends his church to be. Vision is vital. "Where are we headed?" is a valid question. Since the very function of the pastor entails a spiritual gift and a supernatural empowerment, the God-anointed, God-appointed pastor in tune with God should know the vision of the church better than anyone else.

Vision is vital in the dynamic of the church. The wisest man who ever lived put it like this: "Where there is no vision, the people perish" (Prov. 29:18 KJV). The word translated "vision" is found thirty-five times in the Old Testament and means a revelation of what God wants us to be. Not what we are now. What we could be! Its root meaning, according to *Strong's Hebrew Lexicon*, is "to mentally perceive; to contemplate." The word *perish*, appearing nineteen times in Scripture, means "to go back." It is used in Exodus 5:4 to describe those in the wilderness who wanted to go back to Egypt. In Exodus 32:25

this same word is translated "to run wild." In Proverbs, Solomon is saying that where there is no perception of what God desires that we be and/or do, then the people go back without any direction or any purpose. It falls to the pastor to cast the vision before the people of what God wants us to be and where he wants us to go as a church. The pastor's perspective at this point is vital to the church's spiritual success.

The pastor comes from a long line of God-called visionaries. We have been preceded through the centuries by spiritual leaders who saw not what was apparent, but what they could become and what God wanted them to be or do. Joshua and Caleb are certainly two who come immediately to mind. They were among those who went in to spy out the land of Canaan. Their friends returned and saw what was: walled cities and giants in the land. Joshua and Caleb saw what could be and would be if they followed their God-given vision.

Vision is vital. Soon after the completion of Disney World in Orlando, someone asked Michael Vance, at that time the creative director for Disney, "Isn't it too bad that Walt Disney did not live to see this?" Vance quickly replied, "He did see it and that is precisely why we are here today." If this is true for secular organizations, how much more is vision vital for the church of the Lord Jesus? Yes, "where there is no vision, the people perish."

I learned an important lesson in over a quarter century of pastoring the local church. People do not give themselves to need-oriented ministries. Ministries only emphasizing needs do not seem to sustain themselves over time. People give themselves to vision-oriented ministries. They want to be a part of something big, something that will impact the lives of others, something that God is doing and leading. I believe that before every great undertaking, someone has a vision for the task ahead. The football coach has a game plan before the kickoff, a vision of what he wants his team to accomplish. The army commander sees the infantry's strategy before the battle begins. He has a vision of what he wants his troops to accomplish. The artist has a conception in his or her mind before the painting is put on the canvas. What a difference a vision can make. So many churches are just existing, going to meetings, following the schedule, and something is missing. Often, we cannot put our finger on it. What is it? It is vision. Vision is vital. "Where are we headed?" is a valid question for any church member to ask.

As leaders in the church of the Lord Jesus Christ, we have been given a big vision and a large task. Think about it. Jesus challenged a small handful of rag tag disciples, who were basically uneducated, to reach an entire world with the gospel. Talk about a visionary! Their commission, and ours by the way, was not to just go after a few locals, but entire nations all over the world! This vision is even more amazing when we consider the challenge was given to men like James and John, Peter, and Andrew.

They were just some local fishermen from the country-side and were accompanied by men like Matthew from the local IRS office. This should give us hope as pastors. All of us can be a part of the great vision Christ wants to give his church. If they could cast that vision, so can the local church pastor of the twenty-first century. Vision is vital. "Where there is no vision, the people perish." They go back with no real direction or purpose.

PracticalPoints

Now, let's get practical. How can the pastor find God's vision and put it before the people in such a way that they adopt it as their own and the church grows in a way that pleases God, reaches the lost, and builds up the body of Christ? My wife, Susie, and I have had the great joy of seeing the birth of our two daughters, who are now married and have given birth to our grandchildren. Thinking about that birth experience, I am convinced that the birth of a vision is much like the birth of a baby. There are several stages involved. The birth of a child begins with the stage of conception. Then comes gesta-tion. This is followed by the actual birth experience, and in many cases there comes a beautiful word: *adoption*. This is followed by growth, then maturity, and finally reproduction.

The first stage in the birth of a baby, as well as the birth of a vision, is conception. Here the seed of a man connects with the egg of a woman and conception takes place. In the birth of a vision for the church, the seed of that vision comes to take root in the heart and mind of the pastor. For me this happens in the natural flow of my own devotion and prayer life. Conception takes place. God plants the seed of a vision in my heart. It happened with Nehemiah when he heard the report of Jerusalem's broken walls. Upon inspecting his task and catching his vision, he said, "I set out during the night with a few men. I had not told anyone what God had put in my heart to do for Jerusalem" (Neh. 2:12 NIV). Here is conception of the vision. God put it in his mind. It falls to the God-called pastor to develop God's vision for his church. It always begins alone with God. God plants the seed of the vision in our hearts. And one particular person, the pastor, begins to see not what is, but what can be and will be. It is impossible to lead without vision.

The next step in the birth of a baby, or a vision, is gestation. After conception comes a period of time when the vision grows inside us although others cannot see it. Nehemiah said he "told no man." When Susie was pregnant with our daughter, we did not tell anyone for several months. In those first few months she was not showing, but our daughter, Wendy, was growing inside her. This is the way it should be with the pastor when God gives him the vision. There is a gestation period where he lives with it, and it grows inside him. Joseph is a good example of this. God gave him the vision of what he was going to be. And it grew in his heart for a long time, even when he was in an Egyptian jail. But he never lost it and it was eventually birthed. This is the way it happens. The pastor conceives the vision from God for his church, and then it grows in him for a period of time. It gestates. After a while, the people begin to notice he is "pregnant." They see that something is happening in his heart. The vision is growing, gestating, inside him.

Next comes the stage of birth when the baby is actually born, when the vision is brought out for the people to see and hear. Is there any physical joy in life more wonderful than seeing the birth of your own child? You don't give birth and keep quiet about it. You exclaim, "It's a boy!" or "It's a girl!" Once the vision is conceived in the pastor's heart, it is gestated for a proper time through prayer and devotion, and when the time is right, it is birthed. It is revealed to the church. It is out there! Everyone knows it is alive.

In the life of the church, the next stage becomes the most critical of all stages. It is the stage of adoption. It is at this point that the vision either dies of neglect or begins to be nurtured along the way. *Adoption* is a beautiful word. It takes place when individuals who have not personally conceived nor gestated nor birthed a baby take the baby into their homes and hearts as if it were their own and, in fact, it becomes such by all legal rights. It becomes theirs more than anyone else's because they have adopted it. What a beautiful word and how fortunate are people who know this experience. Visions are like babies who are adopted. They are confined to some orphanage of ideas unless they are adopted by the church.

Next comes the stage of growth. Once the vision is adopted, synergy begins to take place. The vision, like the baby, begins to grow. And anyone who has raised a child knows it takes time and money. The growth of our children also causes certain changes to our own lifestyles. As with the growth of children, visions often experience some setbacks along the way. There are accidents and honest mistakes when we are learning to walk and growing through adolescence. But, by and large, the child and the vision continue to grow and grow and grow.

Then there comes a time when the vision reaches maturity. This is an important stage. Here we see all we have hoped for, prayed for, and longed for coming to fruition. I experienced this stage when I walked my daughter down the center aisle of our church and gave her to her husband on her wedding day. At that moment, the conception, the gestation, the growth, and all that went into the raising of that young lady came to maturity. Maturity is a critical time in the life of a vision. There are a lot of churches who saw their vision reach maturity years ago and have never dreamed again.

This brings us to the next step, which is reproduction. This is the stage at which a vision either ceases to exist because it has reached maturity, or it is reproduced into larger and grander visions for the future. We have had the joy of seeing reproduction in our family. Our daughters have dreamed again for us and conceived, gestated, and birthed new members of our family. There are a lot of people in a lot of churches who are the offspring of a group of visionary people who went before them. They sit in pews that vision made possible in bygone days. It is time for the church to dream again, to reproduce the vision, to begin anew the process. And it begins in the pastor's heart with the pastor's perspective.

How does it work? Pastor, it must begin in your own heart as you seek God and his plan for your church. It begins when you, as pastor, make a fresh and new commitment to the Great Commission and the Great Commandment. It begins when you, like Nehemiah and all the others, alone with God find his heart and mind and will for you and your place of calling. Vision is vital for the church, and it begins in the pastor's heart.

Vision has a way of bringing definition to your work and calling. A vision defines the task ahead (see appendix A for more about GuideStone's vision).

PressurePoints

There are several points of pressure that come upon the pastor when visions have a tendency to break down and all too often die. *Leadership* magazine tells the story of a group of pilgrims who landed on the shores of America around 350 years ago. With great vision and courage, they journeyed here to settle the new land. At great risk, they sailed uncharted seas in wooden boats following their vision. In the first year, they established a town. In the second year, they elected a town council. In the third year, the city government proposed building a road five miles westward into the wilderness. In the fourth year, the people sought to impeach the council because they thought the cost of the road to be a waste of public funds. Somehow, these forward-looking people had lost their vision. Not long before, they had the vision to see across oceans. Now, they could not see five miles into the wilderness. Many visions die before they mature because the people get comfortable where they are. There will always be pressure on the pastor to lay aside his vision for the comfort and convenience of church as usual. This is especially true once the church grows, builds her buildings, and begins to mature.

The pastor will feel pressure at virtually every stage of the vision to abandon and retreat to the comfort and confinement within the church walls. If God planted the vision in the pastor's heart, he should not abandon that vision. The challenge for the pastor is to make sure your vision has, indeed, been conceived in your heart by the Holy Spirit and not simply your desire for what you think the church should be or should do.

There are many visions conceived in the pastor's heart that are stillborn before the people because they are not properly gestated. Gestation takes time. Many a vision has never been birthed alive because it was premature. The pastor gets the vision in his heart and instead of living with it, praying on it, and saturating it for months in Scripture to confirm it, he so often tries to give birth to it before he or the people are ready for it. As a pastor, during this gestation period I generally would seek confirmation from the wise counsel of a few close, confidential prayer partners who were leaders in the church. I never wanted to birth a vision that would be stillborn or have to be kept alive on a ventilator, fighting to stay alive. Gestation is the time when the pastor should truly discern if what he is sensing is from God and is God's will for the church. The pastor should not try to force the birth of a vision. There is pressure to do this very thing in so many ways and from so many places. The church will not adopt the vision you put before them unless they truly believe it is from the Lord and that you, their spiritual leader, have adequately gestated it until it is healthy enough to breathe on its own.

Vision is vital. The pastor's perspective for the church, his ability to cast the vision, is critical. However, added pressure comes to the pastor who does not recognize that vision is not enough. It must be coupled with the hard work of the task at hand. It's been said, "A vision without a task is just a dream. A task without a vision is drudgery. But a vision which is coupled with a task is the hope of the church." Think about it. A vision without a task is only a dream. We have all been there. We go to a certain conference and get a vision of what our church ought to be. We come back home but have no task with which to couple the vision, and it becomes only another dream that eventually fades away. On the other hand, a task without a vision is drudgery. Most of us have been there also. We know there is a job to do in the church, and we go about it with no sense of vision or spirit of conquest and it simply becomes drudgery. But when we have a vision from the Lord that has been conceived, gestated, birthed, adopted, grown, and matured, and is coupled with the task God gives us to accomplish it, then it becomes the hope of our church.

PulpitPoints

A vision for the future

Proverbs 29:18

Vision is vital no matter what our lot in life. This is especially true in the life of the church. Many churches are dead, dying, or defeated for lack of a vision and a visionary leader. As mentioned earlier, Solomon said, "Where there is no vision [no concept of what God desires and intends us to be] the people perish" (they go back without any sense of direction). When the pastor discovers God's vision for his church as indicated in this chapter, it will do five things.

- **Vision brings definition.**

  When we truly capture the vision for what God wants us to be and do, it serves to define our task. We are speaking here of a vision statement that in one sentence brings definition to the calling and challenge ahead. Some churches have vision statements that say they are making a "great commitment to the Great Commandment and the Great Commission." This vision defines the task and serves as the lens through which they direct their ministries.

- **Vision brings design.**

  This design is seen in the way the vision is accomplished as outlined above. That is conception, gestation, birth, adoption, growth, maturity, and reproduction.

- **Vision brings dynamic.**

  Not much really happens without vision. There is no dynamic and no motivation. Nothing was happening in Jerusalem until Nehemiah's vision took on definition and design and then it brought a new dynamic to the work. Vision is what brings a dynamic and sense of conquest to the work of the ministry.

- **Vision brings direction.**

  One of the most important things a vision does is provide direction to the ministries of the church. "Where is the church headed?" is a valid question. When vision is there, incarnated into the lives of the members, there is a new sense of purpose and a new sense of direction.

- **Vision brings dependence.**

  Vision will bring a new sense of dependence upon the Lord to the life of the pastor and the church. Visions should be so God-sized that there is no way for them to be accomplished unless God intervenes.

God doesn't see us for what we are now. When he first met Simon Peter, he saw him as a small pebble, but he also saw him as a great rock. He saw the potential that was in him. God sees us and our church not so much for what we are, but what we could be if we receive a vision from him for the work at hand. Vision brings definition, design, dynamic, direction, and dependence to the work of the ministry. "Where there is no vision, the people perish." But when the God-appointed and God-anointed pastor gets his vision from God, it brings definition to the task at hand, design, a new dynamic for the work, a definite direction in which to lead, and a new dependence upon the Lord himself.

PersonalPoints

_____

_____

_____

_____

_____

_____

_____

_____

_____

_____

_____

_____

_____

_____

_____

_____

_____

PersonalPoints

_____

_____

_____

_____

_____

_____

_____

_____

_____

_____

_____

_____

_____

_____

_____

_____

_____

6

The Pastor and His Position

PowerPoints

While it is imperative for the pastor to have a sense of calling to the ministry, he generally will rise or fall on his ability to be a leader in the church to which the Lord assigns him. In chapter 1, we have already noted that one of the words Scripture uses to describe the pastor is the *episkopos*, the overseer. As the under-shepherd of the Chief Shepherd, the pastor is not simply assigned to "feed" the flock of God, but to "lead" the flock of God. It has been my experience in observing hundreds of pastors across the years that this is often their biggest challenge.

Pastoral leadership is the ability to lead by example in such a way that the entire church begins to move together in love and unity toward a common goal. If at any time one wants to know if he is a leader, then simply look to see if people are following. It has been my opinion through experience and observation that in most cases the pastor does not become the pastor-leader of a church, in the truest sense, until the pastor has led a church between three and five years. It takes time to make it obvious that the pastor walks with God, has a servant's heart, and truly loves his people. When this takes effect, leadership begins to come into prominence. Of course, it may happen much sooner, but pastoral leadership must be earned by one who is respected over time by the members of his church.

As a pastor, I always felt that my number one responsibility in the church was to endeavor to "keep the unity of the Spirit in the bond of peace" (Eph. 4:3). Love and unity among the people of God in the local church is the greatest factor in church growth and health. No one can perform this important task as well as the pastor.

PracticalPoints

The ministry of pastoral leadership is a holy and an awesome responsibility not to be taken lightly. In fact, the Bible admonishes those who are church members to remember that the pastors are the ones who "watch out for your souls, as those who must give an account. Let them do so with joy and not with grief, for that would be unprofitable for you" (Heb. 13:17). It is the pastor, and not the church member, who one day will be called upon before the throne to give an account for the leadership of God's people. This very thought was often before my mind in the voluminous decision-making times of pastoral leadership.

Perhaps no other single issue has brought more stress to the pastor and people than the first part of Hebrews 13:17, which was omitted in the verse above. It says, "Obey those who rule over you." Many a pastor has gotten into trouble because he saw himself as a "ruler" rather than a "servant leader." The Greek word that is used here is not the one that often means to rule or reign as a king might do. The word here means to lead or preside and carries with it the idea of being held in esteem. The very same word is translated in Hebrews 11:26 as "esteem." Those who were pastors in this apostolic world were held in high reverence and esteem. People followed them and esteemed them because of the apparent faith and godliness of their lives. Later Peter himself would enlarge on this issue of "ruling" the church by saying the pastor was to lead his people "nor as being lords over those entrusted to you, but being examples to the flock" (1 Peter 5:3).

In a very practical sense, there are several things that go into the pastor's ability to earn the respect of his people in such a way that he can lead effectively. David Hamilton (with whom I shared ministry in three different churches over the course of more than twenty-plus years) and I jotted down some words that characterize for us some important elements of pastoral leadership. At the top of this list is character. I am not speaking here of charisma, but character, that inner being that is rooted in personal conviction and Christlikeness. Nothing lends itself to leadership as much as a personal life of character and integrity in the pastor.

Another characteristic in the pastor that enables him to lead is confidence. Men and women want to follow someone who knows not only who he is, but where he is going. Confidence in the life of a pastor springs from a well-thought-out assignment that has been immersed in prayer.

Compassion is certainly another word that must be incorporated into the life of anyone who desires leadership, especially in the church. This is the ability to truly care and to love people where they are in their own pilgrimage. When the people know the pastor is truly compassionate and filled with love for his people, they will follow him anywhere.

This brings us to the issue of consistency. In order to effectively lead the church of the Lord Jesus Christ, the pastor must be consistent in his own life. He must be one whose life continually and consistently matches his lips. He must follow through on all his assigned responsibilities in a consistent and accountable manner.

Cooperation is another word that should not simply be in the pastor's vocabulary, but should be incorporated into his ongoing leadership style. Specifically, I am speaking here about the pastor's ability to cooperate with those around him in such a way that he makes full use of the important element of delegation. Delegation is one of the signal secrets to the pastor's leadership ability. There are three basic ways most pastors approach this aspect of leadership. Some seem to think delegation means to dictate, so they bark orders and attempt to keep those around them under their thumbs. They always insist on everything being done their way. Those who lead by dictating squelch innovation and creativity among their team. Others act as if delegation means to abdicate. That is, they may assign a task, but they have little passion to follow up and never get around to holding others accountable. Thus, all the big plans and visions end up fizzling out, and things never seem to get done or finished. The wise pastor chooses to delegate instead of choosing to dictate or abdicate.

When I was serving in the position of pastor, I sought to incorporate what I considered to be five very important principles of delegation. The first thing I would say to the busy pastor who needs to learn to delegate assignments in cooperation with his staff or laypeople is to set clear objectives with specific tasks. It is a very difficult thing to delegate a task to someone else unless we communicate to the person a clear objective regarding it. Second, the pastor should pick the right person for the right job. Having the right "go-to person" is essential for effective leadership.

The next important principle of delegation is to be an example yourself. If we want people to cooperate with us and follow our leadership, then we must lead by example. Next, it is vital to hold people accountable. It is at this particular point that much of our delegation breaks down. Accountability is critical in the delegation process and without it, nothing much ultimately gets accomplished. Finally, it is important to give those with whom we work and delegate duties a genuine pat on the back. The elements of appreciation and affirmation go a long way in building cooperation and getting the job done. The wise pastor cooperates with those around him by effective delegation and does not care who gets the credit as long as the job gets accomplished.

Another important factor that lends itself to the pastor's leadership ability is his ability to be contagious in his life and ministry before the people. He should have such winsomeness about him that he begins to reproduce himself in the lives of others. This often takes time and is one of the factors why I believe most of us never truly obtain effective pastoral leadership until we have been in the church a few years.

Then, of course, courage is the key to leadership in most any endeavor. There are many times when being a pastor is a lonely position. From time to time, as a pastor-leader, I would find myself so far out on the limb that unless God came through I was sunk! This strange willingness to fail is always necessary to succeed. There will be times when, in your heart, you know you are right, and you will need courage to lead even in the face of obstacles in your way. People have a way of recognizing this for what it is and respecting it.

Of course, no discussion on these necessities of leadership would be complete without a word on commitment. Our commitment to the Lord, our calling, and his church should be at the forefront of all our decision making and leadership endeavors.

The pastor should give daily attention to his own attitude as the spiritual leader of the church. More than one pastor has allowed his own ego to become his downfall. In the pastorate, the way up is down, and the way down is up! Avoid repetitive use of the perpendicular pronoun in your conversations, sermons, and writings. Instead of saying "I," the wise leader uses "we." The use of the plural pronoun brings people alongside you and builds that spirit of *koinonia* (fellowship) that is vital to leadership success.

PressurePoints

One could write volumes on the pressure points that come to the pastor in the realm of his position as pastoral leader of the church. Any pastor who seeks to truly lead his people will be challenged along the way in some form or another. Incidentally, when criticism would come my way, if I was honest I would, more often than I wanted to admit, find some grain of truth in which I could seek to better myself for the task ahead. Perhaps pastors receive more anonymous mail than those in any other profession. Those anonymous letters are always such a "blessing." I received such correspondence in only one church I pastored, and after a while, I made it my practice not to read it. If someone does not have the courage to sign his or her name, the pastor has no obligation to read what most often is simply the venting of someone's personal prejudices.

Pressure comes in seeking to determine what type of leadership style one will incorporate. There are basically two types of leaders: those who lead by public consensus and those who lead by personal conviction. Those who lead by public consensus will not take a stand on a given issue until they get a feel for what the people are thinking and wanting. They do their opinion polls, so to speak, and come up with a consensus of the people's desires, and then they lead in that way. Those who lead by personal conviction have convictions deep in the fiber of their being about what is right or wrong, and they lead that way, come what may. Those who lead by public consensus lead people to do what the people want to do. Those who lead by personal conviction lead people to do what the people need to do.

It should be obvious that in the church, the pastor should be one who leads by personal conviction. There are worlds of churches that are led simply by public consensus and consequently have little real authoritative leadership nor consistent direction. As a pastor, I saw the necessity to be a leader with personal conviction before my people. However, this is a situation in which it may not be "either-or," but a case of some "both-and."

Let me illustrate. When I would sense the church needed a new direction or new initiative, I would eventually lead out in this on the basis of my own personal convictions derived from what I thought to be God's clear leadership in my heart. However, I did have a few trusted and respected church lay leaders whom I would always bring into my circle of ideas and with whom I would share my heart and request their feedback. (I want to emphasize here the words *trusted* and *respected* lay leaders.) Once I had a sense of confirmation by their respective consensus with my personal conviction, then and only then would I take it to the people. In this way I had the wisdom of many counselors and the support of key lay leaders who would back me in the vision. I might add there was more than one time when this particular approach saved me embarrassment and confusion and maintained my ability to lead.

Another very important element of pastoral leadership is for the pastor never to ask his people to do anything that he himself is not willing to do. One of the greatest principles of leadership to be found anywhere is in the book of Judges when in chapter 7 Gideon has reduced his army to three hundred men, and just before he goes out to fight the Midianites, he turns to his people and says, "Do as I do" (Judg. 7:17). There you have it. Do as I do. This is eventually what the church will end up doing in the long run. That is, they will do as the pastor does. If he is not a personal soul winner, they will not be either. If he does not have a vision of conquest, they will not have one either. If he has a heart full of love, it will be contagious and they will demonstrate love to one another. The church has a way of taking on the personality of the pastor and doing what he does.

Paul alluded to this truth of leadership in the New Testament when he challenged the church to "imitate me, just as I also imitate Christ" (1 Cor. 11:1). We find this truth throughout the Bible. The people did what their leaders did. The Israelites worshiped God because they followed what David did. Influenced by their leader at the time, Jeroboam, the people worshiped golden calves. But then again, they restored the worship at the temple because they followed Hezekiah. There is a strong sense in which this general principle does not speak well of the people in the church. But it does show the importance of what a good and godly leader as pastor can do to influence his church, and through it, touch his world. Pastor, make this your leadership call: "Do as I do."

PulpitPoints

Essentials of pastoral leadership

Acts 13:36

In South Florida, where I pastored for fifteen years, those who owned boats had to periodically bring them into dry dock. There they would be lifted out of the water and the bottom of their hulls would be scraped. Crusty critters called barnacles would attach themselves to the hull of the boat, and they needed to be removed. A boat is designed to skim through the water, but barnacles on the bottom weigh the boat down and cause it not to run at optimum speed and to burn more fuel. In the pastorate all sorts of "barnacles" attach themselves to our lives and ministry and keep us from performing at an optimum level. Therefore, it is good for the pastor, himself, to periodically come into dry dock and remove some of those things that weigh us down in ministry.

There is one verse of Scripture to which I have sought to stay tethered throughout the days of the ministry I have received from the Lord. I find myself going back to it from time to time and reevaluating my priorities. It is found in Paul's sermon to those at Pisidian Antioch when he reminds us that "for when David had served God's purpose in his own generation, he fell asleep" (Acts 13:36 NIV). From this verse emerge four essential elements of pastoral leadership. Paul, the great pastor and leader himself, is saying to us:

- **Be a servant.**

    Of all the things Paul could say about King David, he chose to call him a servant. He said David served. He knew the way up was down and the way down was up! One of the most important elements of pastoral leadership is found in manifesting servant leadership.

- **Be a submissive servant.**

  Paul goes on to say that David served God's purpose. The word here, *boulē*, carries with it the idea of God's irrevocable will, God's calling upon our life. The pastor has a special calling from God, and the pastor is to serve and submit to that calling. The pastor is about something supernatural and should not try to be anyone else.

- **Be a contemporary submissive servant.**

  Paul says that David served God's purpose in his own generation. According to *Thayer's Lexicon*, this word indicates a time span of thirty to thirty-three years. There are often barnacles of tradition that attach themselves to us and keep us from reaching our own generation. The pastor must understand the difference between twenty-first-century methods that can be used in ministry while being careful to maintain the first-century message.

- **Be a contemporary submissive servant with an eternal purpose.**

  Paul says of David that "he fell asleep." That is just a euphemism meaning he dropped dead. And it is appointed once to die and after that comes the judgment. The pastor should never lose sight of the bottom line of ministry, which is leading men and women, boys and girls, to saving faith in the Lord Jesus Christ.

The Lord Jesus is our champion and our example. He was a servant. He humbled himself. He came to "serve God's purpose." He said, "My meat is to do the will of him that sent me" (John 4:34 asv). Was Christ contemporary? He changed everything. He changed the way of worship. He even changed the day of worship. Finally, Christ always kept the eternal purpose before him. Hear Christ say, "For the Son of Man has come to seek and to save that which was lost" (Luke 19:10).

Dry dock. From time to time it is a good place for the pastor to find himself in order that he might be better prepared to fulfill the ministry to which he has been called. Pastor, be a servant. Be a submissive servant. Be a contemporary submissive servant. And above all, be a contemporary submissive servant with an eternal purpose.

PersonalPoints

PersonalPoints

_____

_____

_____

_____

_____

_____

_____

_____

_____

_____

_____

_____

_____

_____

_____

_____

_____

_____

PersonalPoints

7

The Pastor and His Pastorate

PowerPoints

It goes without saying that no one should assume the office of the pastorate with its myriad of responsibilities without a clear and definite sense of calling as discussed in chapter 1. There are times for every pastor when the only thing that keeps him in his place of service is the calling of God upon his life to that particular place at that particular time. Without this sense of divine calling and purpose, it is impossible to function as a pastor. But with it, nothing can keep you from it. God still calls particular pastors to particular pastorates for particular purposes.

The pastorate takes place within the confines of the local, New Testament church. We translate our English word *church* from a compound word in Greek. It contains the preposition *ek*, which means "out of," and the verb *kaleō*, meaning "to call." The church is made up of the called-out ones, and more than 90 percent of its references in the New Testament relate to a particular local body of baptized believers in a certain, specific place. We read consistently of the churches of Asia or the church at Corinth or the churches of Galatia. It is a unique relationship that exists between the God-called pastor and the local group of believers to which God assigns the pastor. The pastor and his pastorate have the opportunity to function together in love and unity with a common purpose to accomplish supernatural things like no other position and organization can do. A spiritual dynamic takes place when God brings a pastor to a pastorate in God's special way and for God's special purposes.

PracticalPoints

This "marriage" of a pastor and a people begins with the initial "flirtation" and "courtship" of the church's pastor search committee and the prospective pastor. For me, this has been a treasured relationship lasting throughout the years of my life. To this day I still count as dear friends men such as Bill Williams and Mervin Greb, who were on that first committee with whom I visited from Hobart, Oklahoma. Members of the committee that came to me from Ada, Oklahoma, a few years later remain my prayer partners to this day. I spoke during the writing of this chapter to Bob Hudson, the chairman of the committee that invited me to Fort Lauderdale in 1978. And the dear people in Dallas with whom I prayed and talked for so long before coming to be their pastor are among the dearest friends of my family to this day. There is something special about this experience.

However, there are several practical points that should be heeded in meeting with pulpit committees. I always made it my policy to never deal with more than one committee at a time. This is important as you keep integrity in the process and guard yourself from getting into some type of a "bidding war." To me it was also important that the committee itself deal with one person at a time. There were times when I heard that a series of candidates was going to come for a visit, one after another. I never was part of such an experience that easily could turn into a beauty contest. I think it is wise for the pastor to deal with a search committee who talks to one person at a time. It is also important for the pastor to make sure he senses that calling as best as he can before he consents to going in view of a call to the church.

Along the way in the process, remember that most search committees move slowly. Don't be overly concerned if they appear in your church to hear you preach and then do not contact you for some time afterward. Patience is the key here. In the initial meeting, I always felt there was a reason God gave me two ears and one mouth. More can be learned by listening closely to what they say than by you dominating the meeting. More than one pastor never got a second visit because all he did was ask questions. Listen to their questions and answer them openly and honestly. Honesty is essential in the process, and this includes the résumé as well. You can learn a great deal by listening. Often if they are asking you about your study habits, it may be because the previous pastor was a superior student and preacher, or it may be because they never saw him as he was "holed up" and separated from the people for most of the week. After listening to them, there are some questions you should ask. For example, you should probe to see what they expect from their pastor, what kind of vision or goals the church might have. Do not fall into the trap of trying to answer the oft-asked question "What is your vision for our church?" Other than a general statement related to the Great Commission or such, how could you possibly know what your vision for their church might be? As we observed in chapter 5, visions take time to conceive and gestate before they are born in such a way that the church adopts them.

On a final word, I made it my policy in dealing with search committees to never bring up the matter of compensation. Some might argue as to whether this is the best approach or not, but I always found that the church did the right thing regarding this without my mentioning it in the process until they brought it up.

One of the keys to success in the pastorate is the pastor's ability to lead his people to discover and use their spiritual gifts. God has sovereignly bestowed upon every believer certain gifts for the work of the ministry through the local church. The church is supernatural not only in its origin but also in its operation as well. I once heard the late revivalist Vance Havner say, "The church has to be supernatural in its operation because anything else could not have existed this long the way most of us are running it!"

Every believer has a spiritual gift (1 Cor. 12:6–7). Many church members do not recognize it, much less exercise it. It falls to the pastor to lead his members to discover their spiritual gifts. While the list of the service gifts in Romans 12:6–8 and Ephesians 4:7–13 is not exhaustive, the list does give examples of the more common gifts that the Lord bestows on his children. Among those listed in Romans are gifts of helps, service, teaching, exhortation, giving, leadership, and mercy. In the Ephesian epistle, Paul lists such gifts as the evangelist, pastor, and teacher. These gifts are never intended to be sought or caught or taught and, surely, not bought. They are Christ's ascension gifts to his church, sovereignly bestowed upon us without merit.

Many resources are available to the pastor to help him in leading his people to discover their spiritual gifts and to put them to use within the church in the building up of the body of Christ. One of the things I taught my people in the pastorate was that personal inclination was a good sign in discovering spiritual gifts. If you have a gift, God will incline your heart toward it, and you will love performing it. For example, I know some with gifts of mercy who love visiting the sick and helping those in need. Another positive indicator of a spiritual gift is public recognition. If you have a certain gift, others will recognize it, the church will use it, and God will bless it. God gifts individual members of his body in order to produce service, provide unity, and promote love.

Let me also say a brief word about common sense. It may be that many of us in the pastorate have fallen upon difficult times for the simple fact that we did not use good common sense in certain situations. The pastor should use two senses: uncommon sense and common sense. Uncommon sense is that sense we put into practice in the faith life. There are times in the pastorate when common sense says a situation is hopeless, and we need the uncommon sense to believe God can make the impossible possible. Elijah used uncommon sense in 1 Kings 17 when he went to the Brook Cherith believing, as God promised, the ravens would bring him food. Two chapters later, after running from Jezebel and falling into depression, he had the common sense to eat and sleep. Occasions often arise in the pastorate when just plain old common sense is the order of the day. At the critical moment of the Jerusalem Conference in Acts 15, twice it says, "it seemed right" to the apostles. They looked at the dilemma of what to do with the Gentile believers, and common sense won the day. Pastor, use uncommon sense. Lead by faith, but also be sensitive enough to know when to use common sense in dealings in the pastorate. It will go a long way in bonding you to your people. Don't be afraid to lose a few battles along the way to win the bigger war.

Many pastors look upon the regular church business meeting as a moment to dread. For sure, it has been the breeding ground for many a church fight. This shouldn't be. When I went to my first pastorate, the church used one of the laymen, a good man well versed in protocol and *Robert's Rules of Order*, to moderate the business meetings. At first, I took a bit of offense to the fact that the pastor was not the moderator. In most instances, this task should be filled by the pastor. However, I found having a moderator was an effective way to function. It freed me, as pastor, to have the opportunity to speak to various issues when and if they came up that I would not have been privileged to do had I been moderating the meeting. The wise pastor will find his way through these issues and will seek to use occasions of church business to unify the congregation and not divide it.

My biggest frustration in writing this book is the necessity of editing out valuable practical matters in order to keep the book a readable and reasonable length. There are so many more practical matters related to the pastor and his pastorate I would like to add. See chapter 8 for a similar discussion on the practicalities related to the pastor and his people.

PressurePoints

Many pastors find themselves in pastorates in which they are expected to be spiritual supermen, always ready to leap tall buildings in a single bound. The pastor is expected to counsel without a degree in counseling. He is expected to manage the financial affairs without a degree in accounting. He is expected to effectively manage all personnel matters without a degree in management. He is expected to take care of all the business without a degree in business administration. He is expected to heal without a medical degree. In addition to all this, some churches expect their pastor to preach like Paul and then simply nod when someone says "What a great deal he has. He preaches a couple of sermons a week, and that is about it."

It will not be long until the pastor has to deal with criticism. It finds its way to us. Sometimes through the grapevine, sometimes through the mail, sometimes face-to-face, but it has a way of getting back to us. I learned a valuable lesson from my deacon chairman in Ada, Oklahoma, years ago. He was a rancher whose grasslands were interrupted by the discovery of oil. Suddenly, his cattle had to find their way around numerous oil derricks to graze day by day. He was a good and godly man who knew the Word as well as anyone in the church and who had the keenest sense of wisdom and common sense of any man I knew. On a given day, there had been a deacon in our church who was causing dissension, and I had had enough of it. I got in my car and drove to the deacon chairman's home, told him the problem, and suggested that we go together and confront this man. I have never forgotten his wise reply, "Now, preacher, early this morning I was out at the ranch checking the wells. I came upon a cow patty all crusted over. It didn't stink at all until I kicked it!" Crude? Yes. But a powerful lesson I never forgot along the years of ministry.

Moses was the object of untold criticism during the wilderness wanderings. But he was wise as the leader of his people. He didn't take it personally. He knew their real complaint was against God. He didn't take it out on the people. Too many preachers use their pulpits to beat up on people when one or a few have criticized them. Finally, Moses took it to the Lord ... and left it there. That is wise counsel for a pastor and his pastorate.

Perhaps the biggest challenge for the pastor in the church is in the realm of effecting change. *Change* is a dirty word for a lot of congregations. There is a sense in which churches are like airplanes. They all have the same purpose and all follow the same laws of aerodynamics. But how different they can be. Some resemble Piper Cubs. They do not carry many passengers, don't get to their destinations as fast as other planes, but they are easy to maneuver and operate. Other churches are like corporate jets, slick and polished. They usually carry only one type of passenger. Everyone on board looks basically the same. Then there are some churches like big B-52 bombers. They are old, out-of-date, and sluggish, so they compensate by dropping bombs on others. And then, there are the impressive super churches, like 747 jumbo jets. They are so large they fit in only a few places. A pilot knows a 747 cannot be turned on a dime. To attempt a 90-degree turn would result in a loss of altitude and air speed. Passengers would tend to panic at such a sudden change in direction. The wise pilot turns the 747 at a 30-degree angle. When it is turning at this proper angle and speed, the passengers do not even notice it.

Most pastors in these days of the twenty-first century find themselves pastoring churches, small and large, that are in need of a change in direction. The wise pastor doesn't turn his church on a dime. He takes his people along with him. Jesus reminded us in Matthew 9:17 that men do not take new wine that is in the fermentation process with its gases still expanding and put it into old, brittle wineskins that have lost their elasticity. If such happens, the skin breaks and both the wine and the skin are lost. Instead, he takes this new wine and puts it into new skins that can expand, and both are preserved. Pastor, the wine is the message. It never changes. The skins are the methods that should be constantly changing. In effecting change in the church, the wise pastor recognizes the difference and does not sacrifice the age-old message when attempting change. He leads his people to the new skins of methodology wisely and winsomely.

PulpitPoints

Never cut what you can untie.

Nehemiah 5:1–19

There was a particular boy on my street when I was growing up whose tennis shoes were invariably laced only halfway up. When his shoelaces knotted, he never took time to untie them. He simply pulled out his pocketknife and cut off the knot. I thought about him recently while reading Nehemiah 5. I came to the conclusion that pastors should never cut what they can untie. They should work through the knots of interpersonal relationships in the church without just cutting them off.

Conflict resolution is important to the body of Christ. Conflict can do irreparable damage. It can tear your team apart, whether you are on the court, in the home, at the office, or in the church.

Among the pastor's highest priorities in the pastorate is "endeavoring to keep the unity of the Spirit in the bond of peace" (Eph. 4:3). Nehemiah, the faithful rebuilder, shows us the way to conflict resolution. The wise pastor in his pastorate knows when it is time to back off, time to stand up, time to give in, and time to reach out.

- **There is a time to back off.**

  Nehemiah was wise enough to know that in conflict resolution there are times when the best thing we can do is back off and give "serious thought" (v. 7) to the situation. When conflicts arise, it is usually best for the pastor to back off initially and listen to his heart and give "serious thought" to the situation at hand.

- **There is a time to stand up.**

  After backing off, Nehemiah then boldly confronts those he believed to be in the wrong. He "rebuked" them (vv. 5–7). Conflict resolution does not mean giving in at all costs. Sometimes the pastor has to "make peace." Jesus pronounced a blessing on the "peacemakers," not the "peace lovers." However, standing up should always follow a time of backing off.

- **There is a time to give in.**

  I can almost hear the conciliatory tone in Nehemiah's voice as I hear him pleading with his people in verses 10–11. He is not showing weakness here. He is showing true strength. In fact, it takes more security to give in than to stand up. Those who resolve conflicts know there is a time to give in and lose a little skirmish or two in order to win the bigger war.

- **There is a time to reach out.**

  In verses 10–13 we read repeatedly the personal pronouns "we" and "us." He is now reaching out to his people. He is building consensus, building bridges to his people. What was the result of backing off, standing up, giving in, and then reaching out? "And all the assembly said, 'Amen!' and praised the LORD!" (Neh. 5:13).

Some pastors are prone to deal with conflict by simply backing off. They never stand up, seldom give in, and do not reach out. Others are known for the way they continually stand up. Still others seek to deal with conflict by only giving in time after time and thus lose their leadership. The pastor who solves conflicts is wise enough to know that timing is everything and knows there is a time to back off. He also knows there is a time when he must stand up for what is right. He is wise enough to know there is also a time of giving in on certain nonessentials. In fact, there is something about that that has a liberating effect. And he does it all in the context of reaching out to his people.

The Lord Jesus is our example. You were once in conflict with him and his purpose and plan for your life. So what did Jesus do to resolve this conflict? First, he backed off. Can you see him in Gethsemane's garden in serious thought and prayer? He backed off and took counsel with his heart. Next, he stood up. Can you see him before Caiaphas, before Herod, before Pontius Pilate, before all his accusers? Then, he gave in. No one dragged him to Calvary. No one pushed him up the Via Dolorosa. Willingly, he laid down his life. Finally, he reached out. Do you see him on the cross? His arms are outstretched, reaching out to you. He died your death, so you could live his life. He is the ultimate answer to all conflict.

PersonalPoints

_____

_____

_____

_____

_____

_____

_____

_____

_____

_____

_____

_____

_____

_____

_____

_____

_____

_____

PersonalPoints

8

The Pastor and His People

PowerPoints

Apart from our own family relationships, few relationships in life are as meaningful and potentially productive as that between the pastor and his people. There is a unique bond in play here that is built on trust and mutual respect. My pastor would often say to me when I was a young man, "Never use your people to build your own ministry. Use the ministry God has given you to build your people." Unfortunately, many of us can point to occasions when the pastor was guilty of using his people and the platform God had given him to promote himself and his own ministry. The calling and gifts of ministry that the pastor have received from the Lord should be used to build up the people to whom he has been divinely assigned and for whom he is spiritually responsible before God. The pastor who refrains from using his people to build his ministry and who uses the ministry he has received from the Lord to edify his people is one who wisely uses the stewardship with which he is entrusted.

It does not take the pastor long to realize that life is about relationships. If, to use a crass term from the business world, one is asked, "What does the church have to 'market'?" The answer in a word is "relationships." Initially, we think that sounds simply superficial. Let me hasten to add that there are only three relationships in life as we have noted in chapter 2: the outward relationship we have with those at church, at work, in the home, or in the social arena; the inward relationship we have with ourselves; and the upward relationship we have with the Father through our Lord Jesus Christ.

The wise pastor realizes that we will never be properly related to one another until we are properly related to ourselves, and this does not happen until we come into relationship with Jesus Christ so that we find our self-worth in him and translate it to those around us. Many a pastor has been trained at the seminary in all the fine points of theology, the biblical languages, homiletics, and hermeneutics only to falter and fail in the pastorate because he could not maintain productive interpersonal relationships. Life in the church, as well as anywhere else, is about relationships.

When I accepted the call to pastor the First Baptist Church in Dallas, I took a month off in the transition from Florida to Texas. I knew I was coming into a situation where some relationships had been strained over a difficult period in the life of the church. At the time, my devotional Bible reading was taking me through Kings and Chronicles. I remember how vividly God spoke to me from the Bible during those days for the task I was to face. When I came to 1 Kings 12:7, I knew I was on holy ground. Rehoboam had become king of the Southern Kingdom, and he sought the advice of some elders, which he did not take. But I did! They said to him, "If you will be a servant to these people today, and serve them, and answer them, and speak good words to them, then they will be your servants forever." When I began ministering at First Baptist Church, I put that verse on my office desk telephone. I placed it in my wallet in front of my credit cards, and I put it on the dash of my car and at my study desk at home. Dozens of times a day for all those years, I looked upon that promise from God. I never answered the phone to speak to one of our people without seeing that reminder "to be a servant to those people and answer them and speak good words to them." And do you know what happened? They became my servants in a mutually beneficial relationship that exists to this day.

Pastor, love your people. Be a servant to them. You are never more like Jesus than when you are washing someone's feet. Never use your people to build your own ministry or kingdom. Always use the ministry you have received from the Lord to build your people. Life is about relationships.

PracticalPoints

There are so many practical ways in which relationships can be built. One could spend an entire volume this size simply on principles that lend themselves to the building of positive, productive relationships. I simply mention a few of the more obvious ones below for your consideration and application.

- **Be approachable.**

People in the pew need to know that they have a pastor who is approachable. Most of them are wise enough to know the pastor's time is his most valuable commodity, but there are times when they need to know they can speak to the pastor. There will always be those who may take advantage of this; who, for whatever their reason or motive, simply want to get close to the pastor. The wise pastor can discern this and not allow it to consume his schedule. But at the same time, a primary principle in positive relationships is in this matter of feeling that the pastor is approachable. And yet, although you want to be approachable, the wise pastor realizes that he can pour his life into only a few people relationally.

- **Be affirming.**

I am convinced one of the greatest motivating

factors in the world is a simple pat on the back. People need encouragement. And they need it from their pastor both publicly from the pulpit and personally in the pew. In order for affirmation to be effective, it must be personal. Never send a word of affirmation through a third party. Give that pat on the back yourself. Affirmation must also be positive. It must also be present. Words of affirmation for something done long ago lose their effect. Affirmation, to be effective, must also be pointed. That is, it should be specific. We should give a pat on the back for something specific. And it should also be passionate. It should issue out of a genuine heart that is moved by the good deeds of others and expresses it in an encouraging way.

During my days in the pastorate, I made it my policy to write on average about five handwritten notes of affirmation a day. On Sundays, I would take note when, for example, one of our ushers went out of his way to seat someone or meet someone's need. By Tuesday, he would find a note of affirmation from me in his mailbox. I cannot tell you how many times I have found one of our men or women in the church who kept one of those notes in a Bible or purse months and even years later.

Affirmation is one of the most powerful things a pastor can do in building relationships with the people.

- **Be appreciative.**

Learn to say thank you. Show your appreciation to others openly and often. Write a thank-you note on the day someone does something for you or sends you a gift for some occasion. It takes so little to be above average at this point. I am continually amazed at how many people— including pastors—do not promptly express appreciation and thanks. It is important in the building and sustaining of positive relationships.

- **Be affectionate.**

Love your people. God has assigned them to your care. Love is something we do. Give yourself to your people. It does not take long before the people have a sense of whether their pastor has a genuine love for them or not. True love, when expressed in word and deed toward others, has an extremely liberating effect, and it has its own way of covering a multitude of shortcomings. Remember, the Good Shepherd has given his life for the sheep (John 10:11). We, then, as his own under-shepherds should pour out our lives in love for them.

- **Be attentive.**

  Know as many of your people's names as possible. Many of us do not remember names because we never really bring focus to this important discipline. Some of us are often introduced to someone and then, within ten seconds of leaving the person's presence, we cannot even repeat the name. Why? We are not listening and not focused. When I am introduced to someone, I will repeat the name to myself in my mind immediately. Then, as soon as I am away from that person, I write his or her name down on a notepad that is always in my pocket. Writing the name and seeing it in print helps seal it in my memory. There is something endearing about hearing your name mentioned from someone like the pastor for whom you have such respect. Jesus said, "My sheep hear My voice, and I know them, and they follow Me" (John 10:27). Pastor, those sheep who hear your voice week by week would like to know that the pastor knows them by name.

- **Be aggressive.**

  By aggressive, I mean be punctual and prompt in the way you answer your phone calls and return your mail. The pastor should always make it his policy to return every phone call the day it is received when at all possible. This has always been my policy. I cannot recall leaving the office without returning every call that same day. Not only is it the right thing to do, but it keeps your backlog from piling up on you. I made it my personal policy to answer every piece of mail when I received it and felt that if someone wrote me about something, then he or she deserved an answer.

- **Be accurate.**

  In relationships, and in all life for that matter, honesty is always the best policy. Tell the truth. We never have to be afraid of the truth. It has a way of always winning in the end. And there is something about truth telling that has a liberating effect on everyone concerned.

All of the above is never more applicable than with the pastor's relationship with his own staff. The pastor should show extreme care and caution in assembling his staff. Check the résumés and references carefully. Due diligence is a must at this point. When asking people to come alongside me in ministry, I would always ask myself during the interview process an important question, "Is this the type of person I could and would entrust my wife and children with in time of need or emergency?" If I did not have a good feeling about this, I would have some reservations about the individual. I always asked a question of all those I interviewed that was phrased something like this: "Do you have any skeletons in your closet that you would not want me to find out about later?" It is amazing how this opens up the conversation and either brings red flags of warning, yellow flags of caution, or green flags of go. Once your staff is in place, there is nothing that builds a team spirit of love and unity like affirmation from the pastor. This should come both publicly and personally. It is up to the pastor to "maintain a spirit of unity in the bond of peace" with his own staff, especially before the people.

The church is in the "people business." The pastor and his people have a unique relationship with each other. Yes, life is about relationships ... especially in the church.

PressurePoints

I own an automobile. Periodically, I take it into the dealership where I purchased it for a regular checkup. My wife and I are fortunate enough to own our home. Recently, we had to do some repairs on the roof because of some rotting wood. We call it preventive maintenance. It was not leaking, but it was about to do so. I have a body and every year I go to the clinic to have a complete physical examination. Much of what goes wrong with my car or my home or even my body does so because of one word: *neglect*. No checkup. No maintenance. No accountability. *Accountability*. Now that is an important word. If it is good for cars and homes and physical needs, why shouldn't it be good for relationships, especially those between the pastor and his people?

It may be that more pastors have faltered and failed at this point than any other. Some feel they should not have to be accountable to anyone for anything. But the wise pastor realizes that he is a man not only in authority, but under authority. Fortunate is the man of God who has a peer in ministry with whom and to whom he is accountable. My lifelong friend, Jack Graham, and I entered into an accountability relationship as teenagers together although we did not even know what to call it. On numerous occasions across the decades, we have held each other accountable in various areas of our lives and ministries.

We all need accountability with others in the outward expression of our relationships. Pastors need a friend with the courage of a Nathan to hold us accountable. We need accountability with ourselves in the inward expression of our relationships. We need to make an honest inventory of our lives and hold ourselves accountable. Ultimately, we need to remember we will all be accountable to God in the upward expression of our relationships.

In anticipation of this day when we will give account to God, there are three important questions I have always had written in the flyleaf of my Bible and that I have always asked myself when I have approached some confusing intersection of life. First, "Can I do it in Jesus' name?" The Bible says, "Whatever you do in word or deed, do all in the name of the Lord Jesus" (Col. 3:17). A second question is "Can I thank God for it?" That is, when it is all over, can I look back and thank God for the decision I made? The Bible says, "In everything give thanks" (1 Thess. 5:18). Finally, ask yourself, "Can I do it for God's glory?" Paul admonished those in Corinth saying, "Therefore, whether you eat or drink, or whatever you do, do all to the glory of God" (1 Cor. 10:31). Many a time as pastor I have saved myself untold grief and potential broken relationships by asking myself these three questions before I acted on my own impulses.

Pastor, be accountable to God and to others.

PulpitPoints

The power of positive, productive, interpersonal relationships

Philemon 1–25

What does the church have to market to a world around us? In a word, relationships. There are only three in life. There is an outward expression; that is, the relationship we have with one another at home, in the office, and in the social arena. There is also an inward expression. This is the relationship we have with ourselves, our own self-worth. Finally, there is an upward expression. This is the relationship we can enter into with the Father through the Lord Jesus Christ. And the bottom line? We will never be properly related to one another until we are properly related to ourselves, and we will never be properly related to ourselves until we discover how indescribably valuable we are to God and come into a personal relationship with him.

The letter of Paul to Philemon is about relationships in the church. It is about the pastor and the people. After Paul's salutation to Philemon, five paragraphs follow, each with a vital element in interpersonal relationships. He reveals to us the importance of:

- **Affirmation of one another (vv. 4–7)**

  Paul begins by giving Philemon a pat on the back. How do you think Philemon felt when he read, "Your love has given me great hope and encouragement because you, brother, have refreshed the hearts of the saints?" (NIV). Affirmation is the greatest motivational factor to be found in interpersonal relationships.

- **Accommodation of one another (vv. 8–11)**

  Paul says that Onesimus was formerly "unprofit-able to you, but now is profitable to you and to me." Here is the synergistic principle of what the business world calls win-win relationships.

- **Acceptance of one another (vv. 12–16)**

  Here Paul deals with the vital and important aspect of forgiveness in our relationships. True reconcili-ation requires a repentant heart on the part of the offending party and a receptive heart on the part of the offended party.

- **Allegiance to one another (vv. 17–21)**

  Paul lets Philemon see he is committed to their mutual friend Onesimus and says, "But if he has wronged you or owes anything, put that on my account." True commitment is one of the missing elements in many relationships today.

- **Accountability to one another (vv. 22–25)**

  Listen to these words in closing, "Prepare a guest-room for me, for I trust that through your prayers I shall be granted to you." When Philemon read this, he must have thought, "Paul is going to come by and check up on me. He is going to hold me accountable!" We all need accountability in our relationships with one another.

Yes, life is about relationships. This is certainly true in the church with the pastor and his people. We will never be properly related to one another until we are properly related to ourselves, and this will never happen until we are in such relationship with our Heavenly Father that we find our identity in the person of the Lord Jesus Christ. Once when someone asked our Lord about the greatest commandment of them all, he put all three of these relationships in his answer: "'You shall love the Lord your God with all your heart, with all your soul, with all your strength, and with all your mind,' and 'your neighbor as yourself'" (Luke 10:27).

PersonalPoints

_____

_____

_____

_____

_____

_____

_____

_____

_____

_____

_____

_____

_____

_____

_____

_____

_____

_____

PersonalPoints

_____

_____

_____

_____

_____

_____

_____

_____

_____

_____

_____

_____

_____

_____

_____

_____

_____

_____

9

The Pastor and His Prayer Life

PowerPoints

There is an important insight for every pastor when the office of deacon is instituted in Acts 6. God gifted the church with the ministry of the deacon in order that the pastor could devote himself "continually to prayer and to the ministry of the word" (Acts 6:4). The pastor has no higher calling than to the ministry of intercession. In fact, prayer and the ministry of the word are inseparable. This is why they are coupled together in Scripture. Prayer without the word of God has no direction. The ministry of the word without prayer has no dynamic. It is the pastor's sacred duty to devote himself to these two things above all else.

A keen biblical insight to this principle is found in Exodus 34:34, "Whenever Moses went in before the LORD to speak with Him, he would take the veil off until he came out; and he would come out and speak to the children of Israel whatever he had been commanded." Pastor, this is our proper order. We have no right to speak to men about God unless, first, we have spoken to God about men. Without going in, or coming out, there is no dynamic or direction. It is prayer and the ministry of the Word. In that order.

The pastor's prayer life has a public dimension, a personal dimension, and a private dimension. When offering public prayer, the pastor should make sure his prayers are personal and pertinent to avoid coming off as pious and pompous. There are some who sound completely different in their diction and inflection when they are praying and when they are otherwise speaking. It behooves us all to remember in public prayer that our audience is not the congregation. I heard it said of a pastor's public prayer that it was "the most eloquent and articulate prayer ever offered to the congregation." The pastor should make sure his public prayers are directed to the Lord and not to his people.

There is also a personal dimension to the pastor's prayer life. Every pastor needs the confidence and support of a small number of prayer partners in whom he can confide and with whom he can pray. Of course, the pastor's wife should be foremost in this regard. I have been blessed with a wife who is truly a woman of prayer and whose prayers have sustained me over and over through the years. As a pastor, I always made sure I had a few select men in the church with whom I shared my heart and with whom I prayed.

The pastor's private prayer is the secret of his life and ministry. Over and over in the Gospels, we find our Lord retreated up onto the mountain or wherever in order to be alone with the Father. If he who never sinned saw the need of private prayer alone with the Father, how much more do we? Jesus instructed us saying, "When you pray, you shall not be like the hypocrites. For they love to pray standing in the synagogues and on the corners of the streets, that they may be seen by men. Assuredly, I say to you, they have their reward. But you, when you pray, go into your room, and when you have shut your door, pray to your Father who is in the secret place; and your Father who sees in secret will reward you openly" (Matt. 6:5–7). Jesus said go into your room or closet. Shut the door. Pray to your Father in secret. He will answer and reward you. No discussion about the ministry of the pastor would be complete without a discussion of the absolute necessity of being a person of prayer.

PracticalPoints

I found it helpful to pray for five families in my church each day. This plan and the benefits found therein are discussed in chapter 3. When the people in the church know they have a pastor who prays, it moves, mobilizes, and motivates them to "go and do likewise."

In a very practical way, I find the following pattern of prayer to be helpful as it guides me through my daily prayer time. For me it has always been a good discipline to have a definite and assigned place to meet God each day. Once there, I have journeyed through my intercession in the following manner:

- **The prayer of confession.**

  This is the place to begin. After all, the Bible says, "The LORD's hand is not shortened, that it cannot save; nor His ear heavy, that it cannot hear. But your iniquities have separated you from your God; and your sins have hidden His face from you, so that He will not hear" (Isa. 59:1–2). The psalmist said, "If I regard iniquity in my heart, the LORD will not hear" (Ps. 66:18). So the place to begin in prayer is with 1 John 1:9 in confession of our sin. Our sin is dealt with on Calvary (1 John 1:7). Our sins are dealt with through continual confession (1 John 1:9). Perhaps there are sins of the tongue, things we have said, that need to be confessed and forsaken. Or sins of action, things we have done. There are also sins of thought. Your mind is like a hotel. The manager cannot keep someone out of the lobby, but he can keep him from having a room. It is not a sin when some thought passes through our minds. The sin comes when we give it a room in our hearts. There are also sins of omission that need to be confessed. These are things we knew to do but did not do. Once we have come clean with God through confession, we are now ready for the next season of prayer.

- **The prayer of thanksgiving.**

Psalm 100:4 tells us we are to "enter into His gates with thanksgiving and into His courts with praise." Thanksgiving is the gate through which we enter into Christ's throne room of prayer. Here we thank him for material blessings. We thank him for physical blessings that have come our way. At this time in prayer I pick out a person or two for whom I am truly thankful and offer thanksgiving for them. We should also pray prayers of thanksgiving for spiritual blessings that have been bestowed upon us. After a season of thanksgiving, we are now ready to enter into his courtroom.

- **The prayer of praise.**

"Enter into His gates with thanksgiving and into His courts with praise." In chapter 1 we noted in our calling that Paul was set apart for service when the church was "ministering to the Lord and fasting" (Acts 13:2 NASB). So much of our ministry time is spent directed at one another or at the lost or needy, and too little is spent in "ministering to the Lord." Tell God you love him. Give God praise. Praise God for one of his attributes: goodness, mercy, patience, or holiness. We thank God for what he does; we praise God for who he is. I have made much use of repeating hymns of praise to Christ during this prayer of praise. I cannot imagine a time of extended prayer without a Bible or a hymnal, for that matter.

- **The prayer of intercession.**

  Now that we have been in the place of prayer for some time, we are ready to intercede on behalf of others. We are now approaching the throne on behalf of someone else. Here we pray for family members, church members, missionaries, friends, political leaders, as well as those who are lost and those who are sick. One of my greatest joys in my own prayer life across the years has been found in praying for those who have spoken against me.

- **The prayer of petition.**

  At this point in our private prayer time, we ask God for anything and everything he has placed upon our hearts. Here we petition God for our personal needs and call upon him with the hidden secrets of our hearts.

- **The prayer of communion.**

  This is the prayer that goes beyond mere words where we are still for a while with an open Bible and listen to that still small voice speaking to our hearts by the Spirit and through God's Word. Be still ... and listen. Jesus said, "My sheep hear my voice and they follow me." Do not rush from the place of prayer. Listen to God's voice.

God answers prayers. Always. Sometimes his answer is direct. That is, we pray and directly see the answer to our prayers. At other times it is delayed. Just because we have not seen the answer yet does not mean we are not in a bit of a holding pattern before the answer comes. There are times when the answer is different. God answers our prayers all right but in a different way than we had anticipated. And then, there are times when they are denied. In other words, God sometimes answers by saying no. But it is always for our ultimate good and for his own glory.

PressurePoints

One of the most prevalent PressurePoints in my own prayer life as a pastor came at the point of the time consumption and the busyness that accompanied my many tasks. More times than I would like to admit, I found myself like many believers who get all ready for the battle of the Christian life by putting on the various pieces of the armor mentioned in Ephesians 6. We clothe ourselves daily with such things as the breastplate of righteousness. We hold in one hand the shield of faith and in the other the sword of the Spirit. We have on our heads the helmet of salvation. Many of us get all dressed for the war but have no idea where the battle is being fought. Where is the battlefield of the Christian life? The very next verse after the list of all our armor tells us, "Praying always with all prayer and supplication in the Spirit, being watchful to this end with all perseverance and supplication for all the saints" (Eph. 6:18). Prayer is the pastor's battlefield. It is here, in the place of prayer, that victories are won or lost. It was in the place of prayer in Gethsemane's garden that our Lord won the battle of Calvary. And it is in the place of prayer where our battle is truly fought.

The pastor needs to be reminded that there are four "alls" in Ephesians 6:18. Our prayer should be comprehensive. We are to pray with "all prayer" as indicated above in the PracticalPoints. Our prayer should be continuous. We are to pray at "all times." Jesus admonished us to "watch therefore, and pray always" (Luke 21:36). Our prayer should also be courageous. That is, we are to pray with "all perseverance." This is close to the heart of what Christ said in Luke 18:1, "men always ought to pray and not lose heart." And our prayer should be collective. We are told to pray for "all the saints." The pastor should feel the same burden as did the great prophet of old, Samuel, who said to his people, "Far be it from me that I should sin against the LORD in ceasing to pray for you" (1 Sam. 12:23).

Prayer is the battlefield of the pastor's life. Pastor, put on the gospel armor ... each piece put on in prayer.

PulpitPoints

Praying for the pastor

Ephesians 6:19

Often, as a pastor, I would have people come to me and ask, "Pastor, how can I pray for you?" Each time I would direct them to Paul's words to the church at Ephesus. He charged them to be watchful with supplication for all the saints "and for me, that utterance may be given to me, that I may open my mouth boldly to make known the mystery of the gospel" (Eph. 6:19). The people should pray that their pastor might have:

- **Freedom in the delivery of the Word of God**

  "That utterance may be given to me." While the pastor may not know how to define nor even articulate what unction is, he certainly knows when he has it and when he doesn't. Freedom in the delivery of the sermon is vital to communicating adequately the gospel message.

- **Fearlessness in defense of the Word of God**

  "That I may open my mouth boldly." There are all sorts of pressures upon the preacher to back off from certain controversial and confrontational issues. The true preacher of the gospel must be fearless in the defense of the gospel message.

- **Faithfulness to the doctrines of the Word of God**

  "To make known the mystery of the gospel." The gospel is a sacred secret, a mystery that the pastor must be faithful in making known to the people.

How better to pray for your pastor than to pray for freedom, fearlessness, and faithfulness in his preaching ministry. As a pastor, I was always humbled by the prayers of my people. Often, as I would go to bed in the evening, I thought about the untold numbers of families in my church whose children prayed for me before their bedtime. I am eternally grateful for each and every one of those prayers. They have sustained me; kept me pure in mind, motive and morals; and have served to enable freedom, fearlessness, and faithfulness in the pulpit.

PersonalPoints

_____

_____

_____

_____

_____

_____

_____

_____

_____

_____

_____

_____

_____

_____

_____

_____

_____

_____

_____

PersonalPoints

10

The Pastor and His Power

PowerPoints

We live in a day when the role of the pastor seems to have taken a renewed interest in his being more of the chief executive officer of the church than in his duties of being the under-shepherd, servant-leader pastor. Some seem to believe that power in the pastorate comes from such things as performance, persuasion, and professionalism. However, all the modern techniques, innovations and business principles can never take the place or substitute for the necessity of divine intervention, the absolute and utter dependence upon the Holy Spirit to work in us and through us. Among the pastor's highest priorities should be discovering where his real power lies. Jesus promised that "we would receive power." When? "When the Holy Spirit has come upon you" (Acts 1:8). Our spiritual forefathers who "turned their world upside down" and planted churches across the world in one generation made much of the filling and power of the Holy Spirit in their lives.

In describing this power, the New Testament word is the same word from which we derive our word *dynamite*. The early church had power. And this power was found in the person and work of the Holy Spirit in and through their lives. They did not have a lot of influence. I often fear that too many of us in our day pride ourselves with the influence that comes our way by being pastors. These apostolic pastors did not have enough influence with the city fathers to keep their leaders out of prison. However, they had something better. They had enough power to pray them out of prison. There is the tendency to falter and fail in the pastorate because we confuse influence with power. All the influence the pastor can muster, all the persuasive words of wisdom, and all his winsomeness can never take the place of power that comes only from the Holy Spirit.

As a young pastor in my early twenties, I discovered this power in the Spirit-filled life: power to pastor, power to pray, power to preach. For me I found it to be wrapped in the words of Paul: "Christ in you, the hope of glory" (Col. 1:27). I awakened to the realization that Jesus Christ was literally alive in my life. I was indwelt with his Spirit. I was led by his Spirit. It was his Spirit that illumined the word to my heart in my study. I was given certain ministry gifts by his Spirit for the edification of the body of Christ. I was anointed by his Spirit. The same Spirit that raised Christ from the dead was dwelling in me! Yes, "not I, but Christ." By God's grace, I have stayed tethered to this reality throughout the days of ministry that God has afforded me.

Like many pastors of my generation, I have been blessed by the modeling of ministry that was found in the late Adrian Rogers, longtime pastor of Bellevue Church in Memphis, Tennessee. He is remembered as one of the leading figures in the Battle for the Bible that took place within American Christianity in the 1970s and 1980s. His name is synonymous with expositional Bible preaching. He left us all a legacy of excellence and integrity in pastoral ministry. But perhaps his greatest legacy to pastors was in his repeated emphasis of the absolute necessity of the Spirit-filled life for the pastor.

The pastor must not seek to find his power in who he knows in high places, how many worldly goods he has accumulated, how many degrees he has acquired, or any such things. The only true and lasting power is in the person and work of the Holy Spirit in the life of the pastor, not simply indwelling him but filling him for service. This is where the pastor finds his true cutting edge. All the education in the world will not suffice for the cutting edge. All the natural ability in the world will not suffice for the cutting edge. The cutting edge is found as we come before God, confessed and clean from sin, and yield ourselves utterly and absolutely to God. Then the Spirit indwells us, fills us, and empowers us for supernatural service for the good of the people we are called to serve and ultimately for the glory of God who called us.

PracticalPoints

We read repeatedly in the book of Acts that the church progressed from the place where they were adding new members to the place where they were actually being multiplied. Thousands of people were being swept into the kingdom of God. Entire cities were being shaken. They were turning their world upside down. We do not seem to see much of this phenomenon taking place today. And yet we have all the modern ingredients. We have technology they did not have. We have modes of travel they never would have imagined. We have all sizes and sorts of church growth manuals. We have at our disposal not only thousands of books on the church and church growth, but all the information on the Internet as well. Yet they were being multiplied, and we are not. Did they have something that we might have lost somewhere along the way in all our professionalism and sophistication of church growth principles? I think so. I believe in a very practical sense it is found in Acts 9:31, which tells us "the churches throughout all Judea, Galilee, and Samaria had peace and were edified. And walking in the fear of the Lord and in the comfort of the Holy Spirit, they were multiplied." Did you catch that? They were "walking in the fear of the Lord." Who is doing that today? How many times have we preached on the fear of the Lord? I am convinced that for the pastor looking for power in his life and in his church, this is the signal issue that can bring about a new and God-honoring power.

This concept of living or walking in the fear of the Lord permeated the atmosphere of the early church. At Pentecost, the Bible records that "fear came upon every soul, and many wonders and signs were done through the apostles" (Acts 2:43). In Acts 5 God disciplines the church, and the Bible says, "great fear fell upon all the church" (Acts 5:11). In Acts 10 Peter takes the gospel to Cornelius and exclaims, "Whoever fears Him and works righteousness is accepted by Him" (Acts 10:35). At Ephesus, Paul preached the gospel, and the Bible records "fear fell on them all, and the name of the Lord Jesus was magnified" (Acts 19:17). This emphasis is on virtually every page of the book of Acts. It is woven through the fabric of the lives of all the apostolic pastors. The early church made much of the importance of "walking in the fear of the Lord." This is where they found their power.

It may be that many twenty-first-century pastors seldom, if ever, make mention of this concept because of a faulty comprehension of its essence. It is not the fear that God is going to put his hand of retribution upon you. Some obviously think of it in these terms. That is, to walk in the fear of God means that if we say something wrong or do something wrong, then God will punish us, put his heavy hand of retribution on us. Thus some think to "walk in the fear of the Lord" means that we must live in constant fright or even constant flight of the terror of this Holy God.

I was fortunate as a young man to have a pastor who taught me to walk in the fear of the Lord. He taught me as a young preacher to walk in the fear of God. It was not to live in an atmosphere where I feared that God might put his hand on me. My fear was that God would take his hand off me! This is the fear of the Lord, not that God might put his hand of retribution on you, but that he might take his hand of blessing and anointing off of you. I believe this is what Paul was coming to when he said to the Corinthians that he feared "that when I have preached to others I might become a castaway" (1 Cor. 9:27 KJV). Paul was concerned that he might live in such a way that God would take his hand off him, put him on the shelf, so to speak, and make him a castaway. I believe I have seen this happen to certain pastors along the way of ministry. It is an awesome thought.

The pastor who finds power in his life and ministry is the one who joins those first-generation pastors walking in the fear of the Lord. Pastor, the most practical application you can make at this point is to live your life in such a way before God that he keeps his hand of blessing and anointing upon your life. Remember, it is "daily bread" of which we are to partake. Yesterday's victories will not suffice for today's commitment.

PressurePoints

As we strive for excellence in all we do as pastors, the pressure often comes in the temptation to become absorbed in professionalism. If we allow it, the position of pastor can become a heady calling. Our place of prominence in the community and so many other factors can weigh into our beginning to think that keeping up with the secular professionalism around us is more important than spiritual power.

Many pastors are gifted with warm and winsome personalities. They can find themselves in positions where their ability to win friends and influence others becomes more a priority than the power of the Spirit. Those who are blessed with these attributes have to be on special guard that they do not forget wherein their true power lies.

The demand for performance is another factor that often gets in the way of our true power. Some members in some churches put added pressure on the pastor to perform when they see other churches with performance factors they consider better than their own. While striving for excellence in all things, the pastor must fight against this performance factor at all costs while remembering his power is in an inward possession, not an outward performance.

The ability of persuasion is an added pressure in the life of many pastors. Some church members have ready access through television, radio, Internet, and the like to almost all the high-profile pastors around the country. Many of these men are gifted with unparalleled preaching abilities and too often are readily and unfairly compared to the local pastor. Those with keen abilities of persuasion in the pulpit are easily susceptible to forgetting wherein their true power lies.

All the personality in the world, all the performance one can muster, and all the persuasive ability to move an audience can never take the place of the dynamic power of the Holy Spirit in the life of a pastor who is totally yielded to Christ and who walks daily "in the fear of the Lord."

PulpitPoints

The proof is in the pudding.

Ephesians 5:19–21

Introduction

"The proof is in the pudding" is a familiar phrase. It is actually an abbreviation of the phrase "The proof of the pudding is in the eating." It simply means that the true value or quality of something can only be judged when it is actually put to use. That is, it is the result that counts.

We have a command in Scripture to "be filled with the Spirit" (Eph. 5:18). Literally translated the command says, "All of you must always keep on being filled with the Spirit." How can we know we are being filled with the Spirit? How will others know? Some would have us think it is in the reception and use of certain gifts of the Spirit. Scripture teaches quite the opposite in the very context of this command. There is an inward evidence, an upward evidence, and an outward evidence. Yes, the proof is in the pudding!

- **An inward evidence (v. 19)**

   What is the inward evidence of the Spirit's filling our lives? "Singing ... making melody in your heart to the Lord." Do you want to know if you are being filled with the Holy Spirit? You will have a song in your heart. Buddhists may have their impressive temples, but they do not have a song in their hearts. Hindus may have their mantras, but there is no song in their hearts. Islam might pride itself in its morality, but where is its song?

   Notice that we are not making rhythm in our hearts. That appeals to the flesh. Nor do we make harmony, which finds its primary appeal in the soulish realm of our emotions. But we make melody, which appeals to our spirit. And note, the melody making is in our hearts, not necessarily in our mouths. Like Paul and Silas in a Philippian jail, we may be in difficult straits, but there can still be a song in our hearts even at midnight.

- **An upward evidence (v. 20)**

  What is this upward evidence? "Giving thanks always for all things to God." The one who is being filled with God's Spirit is one who is thankful for all things. He or she has an attitude of gratitude. We cannot stay filled with the Spirit without being in a spirit of thankfulness to God for all things.

- **An outward evidence (v. 21)**

  There is finally an outward evidence found in our relationship with others. "Submitting to one another in the fear of God." What is this outward evidence? Submission, each of us esteeming others as better than ourselves. This was never more evidenced than in the Upper Room when our Lord himself became the servant of all and washed the others' feet.

Conclusion

Therefore, what is the proof that one is genuinely being filled with God's Spirit? Our command is to be "filled with the Spirit" (Eph. 5:18). In the Greek text there is no period after this verse. It flows right into the next three verses, which pose to us that the proof is in an inward evidence (v. 19). We will have a song in our hearts. It is in an upward evidence (v. 20). We will be living in a spirit of thanksgiving to God always. And it is in an outward evidence (v. 21). We will live in mutual submission. Yes, the proof is in the pudding!

PersonalPoints

PersonalPoints

11

The Pastor and His Privilege

PowerPoints

It is to the pastor that God has given the privilege to stand in Christ's stead and administer the two ordinances that he has given the church: baptism and the Lord's Supper. I have never stepped into the baptismal waters to baptize a new convert or stood at the communion table to pass the bread and the cup that I have not considered it an awesome privilege and a sacred service.

"Ordinance" is a term we use in ecclesiological circles that refers to a religious rite ordained or established by the Lord Jesus Christ. There are marks of an ordinance that are important to remember. One, it is a divinely instructed, outward symbol that presents the great truth of the gospel and the personal relationship of an individual with the Lord Jesus Christ. Two, it is accompanied by a divine mandate to observe it in perpetuity. Thus we see in baptism the beautiful picture of the gospel in the death, burial, and resurrection of the Lord Jesus, and in the Lord's Supper we see pictured his broken body and shed blood for the remission of our sins.

Christ has invested these ordinances in his church to be administered under the church's authority. The

Baptist Faith and Message Statement states, "Christian baptism is the immersion of a believer in water in the name of the Father, the Son and the Holy Spirit. It is an act of obedience symbolizing the believer's faith in a crucified, buried, and risen Savior, the believer's death to sin, the burial of the old life, and the resurrection to walk in newness of life in Christ Jesus. It is a testimony to his faith in the final resurrection of the dead. Being a church ordinance, it is prerequisite to the privileges of church membership and the Lord's Supper. The Lord's Supper is a symbolic act of obedience whereby members of the church, through partaking of the bread and the fruit of the vine, memorialize the death of the Redeemer and anticipate His second coming."

It is important to note that the ordinances are not sacraments. They carry with them no measure of saving grace in and of themselves. They are not sacraments; they are symbols. They are symbols, pictures of the gospel. The ordinances are not pathways to salvation but pictures of our salvation. They are metaphorical and not magical. These two beautiful pictures of Christ—baptism and the Lord's Supper—are the outward expressions of the inward experience of the believer. It is among the pastor's highest privileges and responsibilities to administer them in a worthy manner and with a reverent and God-honoring spirit as a testimony to the Lord Jesus Christ and his sacrifice for sin.

PracticalPoints

In observing these ordinances, let's note their practical meaning, their mode, and their message.

Initially, we will examine the meaning of the ordinances. Baptism, while not necessary for salvation, is vitally important to our Christian growth. In the book of Acts, as soon as we see new converts come to Christ in saving faith, they were immediately baptized. There is something about this means of identification with Christ that launches us into our Christian growth. When we are converted, God gives us light to be baptized. If we do not obey the "light" we have, how can we expect to get more light and grow in Christian grace? Upon embracing the gospel, the Ethiopian eunuch in Acts 8 asked, "There is water, what keeps me from being baptized?" Philip immediately baptized him. In Acts 10, the Roman Cornelius and his family were converted and immediately baptized. In Acts 16, the business executive, Lydia, was baptized right after her conversion. Later, in the same chapter, the Philippian jailor was gloriously saved and immediately baptized.

The meaning of baptism is portrayed in the picture of the death, burial, and resurrection of Jesus Christ and our own death to the old life and resurrection to walk in our newness of life (Rom. 6:4). The new believer should be baptized as soon as possible after conversion as a confession of faith. When one comes to Christ, there is first conviction (Acts 2:37), then conversion (Acts 2:38), and this should be followed by confession (Acts 2:38b). Baptism is the means of the new believer's confession of faith in Christ.

Baptism is to the believer what the wedding ring is to the married person. When my wife, Susie, and I were married on July 24, 1970, she placed a gold wedding band on my finger. I have worn it every day since then. It gives testimony to everyone I see that I am married and have made a commitment to her. Had she given me that ring two months before our marriage, I could have worn it but without the meaning it had after July 24. And so it is with baptism. There are some who have "put on the ring" before their commitment to Christ, who have been baptized before their conversion, but it does not mean what it is intended to portray until we are baptized subsequent to our salvation experience. Only then can we truly show the world that we are identified with Christ in His death, burial, and resurrection and are walking in a new life with him.

Like baptism, the Lord's Supper has a solemn meaning. It is a sacred time when the church comes together to remember the Lord Jesus Christ and his sacrifice on the cross to forgive our sin. The bread brings us to remember his body, which was broken, beaten, and battered for us. The cup, red and rich, serves to remind us that "in Him we have redemption through His blood, the forgiveness of sins, according to the riches of His grace" (Eph. 1:7). There is no saving grace in the act of digesting the wafer or in drinking the cup any more than the waters of baptism will wash away a single sin. The meaning of the ordinances is in the beautiful picture of our Lord, which they so perfectly present to us as a wonder and to the world as a witness.

We will now turn our attention to the mode of the ordinances. What is the proper mode of New Testament baptism? When we read of baptism in the Bible, the Greek verb used to describe it is *baptizō*, which appears in the New Testament more than seventy times. The word means to plunge, to dip, to submerge, to put under. This word is extensively found outside the New Testament in Greek literature. There, it is often used in connection with those who suffer shipwreck and sink and perish under the ocean waves and waters. The story is told of an ancient Greek sea captain whose vessel was taking on water and going down. He sent out an ancient mayday message saying "*baptizō, baptizō*," translated, "I am sinking, I am sinking!" The word means to immerse or bury.

The mode of baptism we find in the meaning of the word and in the experience of the New Testament is that of immersion. We read in Acts that baptism required "much water." For example, "Now John was baptizing at Aenon near Salim, because there was much water there" (John 3:23). In Acts we read that when Philip baptized the

Ethiopian, he "went down into the water" and baptized him (Acts 8:38). New Testament baptism is pictured by Paul as a burial. In Romans 6:4 he says, "Therefore we were buried with Him through baptism into death, that just as Christ was raised from the dead by the glory of the Father, even so we also should walk in newness of life." And at Jesus' own baptism, we read that he "came up immediately from the water" (Matt. 3:16). I have never understood why, if he was simply sprinkled with water, he would have gone down into the river and come up out of it?

In our Baptist tradition, it is crystal clear that the mode of baptism was and remains that of immersion. And it should always follow salvation and not precede it. It is the outward expression of the inward experience of the new birth in Christ Jesus, our Lord. It is for this reason that I made it my practice to make clear this truth while in the baptismal waters with a new convert. I would say something like the following: "Bob, are you following Christ in baptism because you are confident that you have taken him to be your own personal Savior?" At this point the candidate for baptism has the opportunity to publicly express his confession with either an affirmative word or a short testimony of his salvation. At this point I continue, "Then, in observance of your faith in the Lord Jesus and in obedience to his command symbolizing the death and burial and resurrection of our Lord, I baptize you, my dear new brother in Christ, in the name of the Father, the Son, and the Holy Spirit." As I lean him back under the water, I would often say, "You are buried with Christ in baptism unto death" and then, as he came up out of the water, I would conclude, "And risen to walk in newness of life!"

The mode of the Lord's Supper is equally clear in Scripture. It, like baptism, is expressly symbolic with no accompanying saving grace attached. The bread is to be unleavened bread, which is bread made without yeast. Yeast in the Bible is always a picture of sin. We remember our Lord's warning to beware of the "leaven of the Pharisees" (Matt. 16:6). Paul, instructing the Corinthians and us, says, "Do you not know that a little leaven leavens the whole lump? Therefore purge out the old leaven, that you may be a new lump, since you truly are unleavened. For indeed Christ, our Passover, was sacrificed for us. Therefore let us keep the feast, not with old leaven, nor with the leaven of malice and wickedness, but with the unleavened bread of sincerity and truth" (1 Cor. 5:6–8). Since Christ is pictured in the bread of the Lord's Supper and since he knew no sin, it is important that the bread of the communion table be unleavened, without yeast, lest the beautiful picture be perverted.

The cup of the communion table presents a challenge for some. Should the cup contain merely grape juice or fermented wine? While many believe the biblical admonition is unclear at this point, there are some important factors to consider. I find it highly interesting that in the four accounts in the New Testament that give light and focus upon the Lord's Supper, not a single one of them uses the Greek word for wine (Matt. 26:26–39; Mark 14:22–26; Luke 22:19–20; 1 Cor. 11:23–26). While not making a large case for this, I personally am intrigued at this point. In those four instances the Bible simply speaks of the fruit of the vine or the cup. In order for the grapes to become wine, they must ferment, which is a nice word for rot. Since Christ's blood is pure and without sin, could Scripture be encouraging us to simply use the fruit of the vine in order to picture the pure blood of our Lord Jesus Christ, which was uncontaminated by any sin of his own?

The ordinances that Christ has left the church are symbols, not sacraments, and thus their mode is important as we portray him through the elements. Baptism's proper mode is by immersion to picture his death, burial, and resurrection, and our own death to the old life and resurrection to walk in newness of life. The proper mode of the Lord's Supper's is to be observed by using the proper elements of the bread and the cup to symbolize his body and blood broken and shed for our redemption.

Finally, as we think practically about the ordinances, we turn our attention to their message. They have been given to us, the church, in order to remember Christ and his suffering and sacrifice for us. While the pastor preaches sermons weekly from the pulpit, the ordinances are sermons that every believer "preaches." When Paul instructs us regarding the Lord's Supper in 1 Corinthians, he reminds us that we "proclaim the Lord's death till He comes" (1 Cor. 11:26). The word translated "proclaim" in this verse is *katangellō*, which means to preach or to proclaim a message. Every time a believer is baptized or partakes of the Lord's Supper, it becomes a sermon he or she preaches, which gives testimony to the saving grace of Christ. The message is clear and beautifully portrayed in baptism and the Lord's Supper. Christ is King! He was crucified, buried, risen, living, and coming again! And when we are baptized, we look back to his death and resurrection, and each time we come to the Lord's Table we not only look back but forward as well as "we proclaim the Lord's death until He comes!"

PressurePoints

There are some obvious points of pressure that come in the preparation and administration of the ordinances.

As the pastor counsels those who are candidates for believer's baptism, it is important, even imperative, that he make sure they have had a born-again experience of salvation. Many an unbeliever has passed through the waters of baptism without a preceding genuine conversion experience and has thus lived with a false sense of security in the aftermath. The pastor must be careful and cautious, as best he can, that the candidate is a true convert. He must also make it clear in his baptismal counsel that the waters of baptism will never wash away a single sin. Only the blood of Christ can do this.

There is much confusion in the minds of many as to whether baptism is a part of salvation. Much of this stems from an improper interpretation of one verse, Acts 2:38, which reads, "Repent, and let every one of you be baptized in the name of Jesus Christ for the remission of sins; and you shall receive the gift of the Holy Spirit." Along the way of ministry, many pastors will be pressured to explain this verse and its apparent aberration of the contention that baptism is not necessary for salvation. For centuries there has been confusion and controversy over this verse. The key to understanding what this verse is saying is found in a small Greek preposition that our English Bibles translated as "for." The word is *eis*. In some verses of Scripture this same word is translated "for" or "in order to" and in other verses as "because of." It should be read in Acts 2:38 as "because of." In our everyday English vernacular when we may say "He was executed for murder," do we mean "in order to" or "because of?" Or if we state "He has been rewarded for good grades," do we mean "in order to" or "because of?" Read Acts 2:38 again in this light and it becomes clear when you consider the overarching teaching of Scripture that Peter is saying that we should be baptized "because of" the fact that our sins have been forgiven.

In the New Testament use of this preposition, its meaning becomes even clearer. For example, in Matthew 12:41 the Bible records that "the men of Nineveh will stand up at the judgment with this generation and condemn it, for they repented *at* the preaching of Jonah; and now one greater than Jonah is here" (NIV, italics mine). The word translated "at" is that same Greek preposition found in Acts 2:38. Obviously, the Ninevites repented "because of" the preaching of Jonah and the men and women who were converted in Acts 2 repented and then were baptized "because of" the fact that their sins had been forgiven.

When we come to the Lord's Supper, there is pressure in understanding what exactly the apostle means when warning that whoever eats the bread and drinks the cup in an "unworthy" manner will be guilty of the blood and body of our Lord (1 Cor. 11:27). He also says, "For he who eats and drinks in an unworthy manner eats and drinks judgment to himself" (1 Cor. 11:29). Many think we are being warned that if any of us are "unworthy," then we should not partake of the Lord's Table. This raises the question, who of us is worthy? Apart from Christ we are poverty stricken, spiritually speaking. A careful reading will reveal that, thankfully for us, an adverb is in play here and not an adjective. If we were talking about "unworthy" in the sense of an adjective, it would be referring to a noun or a person. It is an adverb that modifies a verb and thus speaks of the way a certain thing is done and not the worthiness of the person who does it. This admonition does not have anything to do with our personal worth. It has to do with the way in which we administer this memorial meal. Everything about it should be done with deep reverence and respect from the preparation to the distribution, from the music to the message. As a pastor, I thought it important when we partook of the Lord's Supper to make it the central part of the worship service and not something that seemed tacked on hurriedly at the end or beginning of the worship experience.

There is also pressure as to who is invited to the table. Some believe it is for local church members only and others should be excluded. This debate is referred to as closed communion versus open communion. I believe it is safe to say that most Bible-believing pastors have taken the position that since it is the Lord's Table, all born-again Christians who have been obedient to believer's baptism should be welcomed. After all, it is the Lord's Table and not ours. God will give the wise and discerning pastor leadership at this point.

Another issue comes at the pressure point of how often to observe the Lord's Supper. In a sense, Scripture leaves this a bit veiled in mystery and without clear direction. It simply says, "As often as you eat this bread and drink this cup" (1 Cor. 11:26). It also says, "Now on the first day of the week" (Acts 20:7) but does not specifically indicate that this should mean every single Sunday. To observe the Lord's Supper too often could cause it to lose something of its mystery and importance. To observe it too infrequently can lend itself to the loss of its importance and significance. In Baptist circles, it is generally observed quarterly and in some cases monthly. If I were still in the pastorate and had it all to do over again, I would celebrate the Lord's Supper much more frequently than I did. The wise pastor will find his way through this issue and appreciate the dynamic impact the Lord's Supper can have upon his people and church when done in such a way that brings honor and glory to Christ who said, "Do this in remembrance of Me" (1 Cor. 11:24).

PulpitPoints

The Lord's Supper

1 Corinthians 11:23–28

We have at our home an old family photo album. You could begin to thumb through it and, most likely, it would mean little or nothing to you. My old home place where I grew up is in there: the little frame home with a white, picket fence. When I look at that picture, it conjures up memories of the scar I still carry on my leg. My dad told me not to climb on that fence, and in disobedience I tried it and will bear on my body the marks of that fence forever. The little three-room house, behind the main house, where I took my new bride to live is in that album. It might mean nothing to you, but when I look at it, a myriad of memories of joy and happiness from our early days of marriage flood my mind and heart.

Just as my own family album brings so many warm and wonderful memories to mind, so does the eating of the bread and drinking from the cup for members of God's forever family. As you partake of the elements in communion, it should call back to memory a vivid experience for you. This is why the Lord's Supper is only for members of Christ's family who have been born into his family by grace and through faith.

The Bible says when you share in the Lord's Supper that you "proclaim the Lord's death" (1 Cor. 11:26). The word *proclaim* translates the Greek word *katangellō*, which means to preach or to proclaim. Every time you partake of the Lord's Supper, you are preaching a sermon by retelling the story of the Cross. The two ordinances, baptism and the Lord's Supper, are sermons you preach about the substitutionary, vicarious, voluntary death of our Lord Jesus Christ. So you are preaching a sermon with four points.

- **A word of explanation (v. 23)**

  An ordinance is a ceremony the Lord commanded his church to observe in this dispensation of grace in which the gospel is pictured metaphorically. In baptism, Christ's death, burial, and resurrection are pictured, as well as our own death to sin and self and "resurrection to walk in newness of life." In the Lord's Supper, Christ's broken body and shed blood are pictured in the taking of the bread and the cup. They are given to us as pictures in order for us to remember him and examine our own lives.

- **A word of exaltation (vv. 24–25)**

The Scripture says, "When He had given thanks He broke the bread." How prophetic. No one took his life from him. He laid it down. The Cross was no accident. We do not take the Lord's Supper to remind him, but to remember him. Thus, we are a thankful people, full of praise and exaltation unto him.

- **A word of expectation (v. 26)**

The Lord's Supper is not just an acknowledgment of his physical absence, but it is an anticipation of his promise to return: we do show the Lord's death, until he comes! We are living now in the "great until."

When I travel, I carry my wife's picture with me and often put it on the nightstand in the hotel room. However, I do not do that when I am at home. Why? I have her physical presence with me there. Christ's promise to us is that one day he is coming back and we are going home. Now, we put his picture out at the communion table through the bread and the cup, but there is coming a day when he will seat us at the banquet table. But for now, we live in expectation of his coming and remember him at his table.

- **A word of examination (v. 28)**

  Paul said, "Let a man examine himself, and so let him eat of the bread and drink of the cup." This word, *examine*, translates the Greek word *dokimazō*, which is used of one in a fabric store who stretches and tests the material before the purchase. We should not come to the Lord's Table without coming clean before him in our hearts and examining our lives before him.

Jesus said, "Remember me." The Lord's Supper is Christ's own "photo album" for his family. At the Lord's Table, we remember what he has done for us on the cross. It means something to us as members of the family because it calls to memory how Jesus "who knew no sin [became] … sin for us, that we might become the righteousness of God in Him" (2 Cor. 5:21). This is the Lord's Table. He invites you, and when you sit there, you begin to preach a sermon. You do "proclaim the Lord's death till He comes!"

PersonalPoints

_____

_____

_____

_____

_____

_____

_____

_____

_____

_____

_____

_____

_____

_____

_____

_____

_____

PersonalPoints

12

The Pastor and His Passage

PowerPoints

Traditionally, in our Bible-believing churches, the pastor's passage into vocational service is through the door of ordination to the gospel ministry. In the New Testament church, there are two offices that are set aside for ordination and the laying on of hands. These are the office of minister and the office of the deacon (Acts 6:5–6; 13:1–4; Phil. 1:1; 1 Tim. 2:7; 3:1–13; 4:13). The ministry of the pulpit and the pew, the prophet and the people, are joined together in ministry in Christ's church. They need each other. They complement each other. Dr. W. A. Criswell, longtime pastor of the First Baptist Church of Dallas, used to say they were like a pair of scissors. Neither blade was very effective without the other. But when they were together, they could cut through any situation or circumstance. They serve to keep each other sharp.

These two offices, the pastor and the deacon, are to be affirmed by the local church. We have a biblical basis for the minister with the election of Matthias in Acts 1:15–26. We also see this as we follow Paul and Barnabas on their first missionary journey and find that they "appointed ['ordained' in the King James Version] elders in every church" (Acts 14:23). For the deacon, our biblical basis for this election and ordination is found in Acts 6:1–6 when the early church wisely appointed the deacons to serve the people in order to maintain unity and so that the apostles could, in Luke's words, "give ourselves continually to prayer and to the ministry of the word" (Acts 6:4).

The deacon gets his name from the Greek word *diakonos*. It appears thirty times in the New Testament and only three times is translated "deacon." The overwhelming majority of times we find the word, it is translated "servant." In the PulpitPoint later in this chapter, more detail is given regarding the instigation, initiation, integration, and inspiration that accompanies this God-given ministry to the pastor and the local church. I have been blessed across the decades with hundreds of good and godly deacons who have served the church and haven been an inspiration to me personally. It should be noted that nowhere in Scripture does the idea of a board of deacons appear. A type of ruling board of deacons, like that of a corporation, is foreign to biblical truth and reality. As we have observed in chapter 6, God has ordained that the pastor be the spiritual leader of the church. God, in infinite wisdom and divine direction, put these two offices together to serve his church. In the churches I have been privileged to pastor, the deacons have always referred to themselves as a fellowship of deacons. This

New Testament term, fellowship, is much more descriptive of the office and ministry of the deacon.

PracticalPoints

Ordination to the gospel ministry is practical in
many ways. To begin with, it is biblical and the service
of the laying on of hands is found throughout the New
Testament. In Paul's last two letters to his son in the ministry, Timothy, he says, "Do not neglect the gift that is
in you, which was given to you by prophecy with the
laying on of the hands of the eldership" (1 Tim. 4:14).
And in 2 Timothy 1:6 he challenges Timothy to "stir up
the gift of God which is in you through the laying on
of my hands." The laying on of hands in ordination is
a symbolic recognition of one's call to service and one's
particular giftedness for such. In no way does it signal
any sort of mystical conveyance of power or authority.
It serves to simply affirm one's calling and serves as a
recognition by the local church of its responsibility of
support and prayer for the individual. It is the church's
way of saying "We recognize your calling and gifts and
pledge our prayers and support to the ministry you have
received from the Lord."

Present-day civil law also brings a very practical
element into ordination to the gospel ministry. I have
pastored in a state that required all ministers to bring
evidence of an ordination certificate in order to be

authorized to perform weddings in the particular county and state. Those serving as military chaplains must also give evidence of ordination to the ministry. Ordination is also the most evident way for the Internal Revenue Service to determine who is legitimately treated as a minister and who is not.

It falls to each local church to properly carry out the ordination procedures. The candidate for ordination to the gospel ministry should exhibit a clear calling to the ministry and should hold deep convictions regarding the Scripture and a working knowledge of the main doctrinal truths of the Bible and the church. The procedure should begin with a meeting between the pastor and the candidate who desires ordination. Assuming there is a confirmation by the pastor, the candidate next should come before an ordination council that is appointed by the church, where he is duly questioned as to his conversion, baptism, church membership, call to ministry, doctrinal convictions, personal integrity, and other such appropriate and applicable issues. The pastor and council then make a recommendation for ordination and a time for the ceremony is determined. At the time of ordination, there is usually a testimony from the candidate, a word of confirmation from the ordination council, a charge to the candidate, a charge to the church, a pastoral prayer, and the laying on of hands that serves to symbolize, as it did in the early church, that the individual is set aside (1 Tim. 4:14) for the ministry.

The process of ordination of the deacon follows a similar pattern. Usually, there is a committee appointed from the deacons that nominates future candidates to the office of deacon for service. Some churches have open church nominations or elections, but I have never been an advocate of this because the scriptural qualifications are sometimes overlooked in favor of such matters as popularity or standing in the community. My own pastor, W. Fred Swank, who pastored the Sagamore Hill Baptist Church in Fort Worth, Texas, for forty-three years, had only seven active deacons. And this was in a church with more than five thousand members. In his words, "The Bible says pick you out seven men among you and that is what I did!" Now, it worked for him because of his long tenure and the total trust and love of his people, almost all of whom he had won to Christ either personally or from the pulpit. (Parenthetically, while he taught me how to do a lot of things in ministry, he also taught me how not to do a lot of things!) Whatever the local congregation's process, the deacon should be tested by tenure in the church and examined by a deacon selection committee before being presented for church approval and ordained to the office.

I would like to add one other practical observation on the point of deacon fellowship. The first two churches I pastored had lifetime deacons who once appointed were there forever. My last two churches had a rotation system in which every three years the deacons rotated off service on active fellowship and then returned in a future year after meeting with the selection committee. I strongly urge this latter process for any pastor. Many a deacon was one kind of man when he was age thirty-five and a very different kind of man when he was sixty-five. The rotation system keeps us from taking our task for granted, and it brings credibility and accountability into the ministry of the deacon.

PressurePoints

There are certainly pressure points that come in the process of ordination. One of the obvious ones is in the fact that the minister might subtly develop a tendency to begin to think that his ultimate source of pastoral authority lies in his ordination by the church. As noted in chapter 1, it is the Holy Spirit who sends a man into ministry, and it is the church that recognizes this and releases him to do the work God has called him to do within the framework of Christ's local church. Pastor, always remember your sense of pastoral authority comes from God's call upon your life and the confirmation of your church and not upon a public ceremony of ordination.

Finally, and I speak from experience at this point, the pressure that comes upon the pastor in the ordination of deacons comes at the point of allowing certain men to serve who are not scripturally qualified. The pastor should seal in his mind forever the warning the great apostle gave to his own son in the ministry, Timothy, when he said, "Do not lay hands on anyone hastily" (1 Tim. 5:22). Many a heartache has come to many a minister because someone was hastily ordained to the holy place of service as a deacon and was not spiritually mature or scripturally qualified. It sometimes takes a very good and godly deacon to be qualified. Pastor, resist the pressure to ordain men as your deacons unless they meet the qualifications laid out in Acts 6:1–6 and 1 Timothy 3:8–13. Allow the Lord to lead you to men in your church with these characteristics and qualifications, and you will have a supernatural gift in the performing of your ministries together for God's glory and the church's good.

PulpitPoints

The deacon ordination

Acts 6:1–7

One of the beautiful gifts the Lord has given the church is the ministry of the deacon. One needs to go back almost two thousand years to the church in Jerusalem to see what brought about this unique and God-ordained office of service. We find here in the birth of the deacon its instigation, its initiation, its integration, and its inspiration. To begin with, we observe:

- **The deacon's instigation (vv. 1–2)**

  By the time we reach Acts 6, we find the church exploding, literally multiplying, in numbers. The ministry of the deacon was born out of a problem. The Hellenistic Jews (those Greek speakers from other nations) in the early church felt that the apostles were showing favoritism to the Hebraic Jews (those native of Palestine). Jealousy in the church began to lift its ugly head. Thus the office of deacon was born out of a potential problem, and its express purpose was to bring peace, love, and unity to the church. Interestingly, when the apostles appointed the first seven deacons, they all had Hellenistic names. This showed incredible wisdom on the part of the leaders of the early church. The deacon's very instigation was in order to maintain unity in the church.

- **The deacon's initiation (v. 3)**

  There were certain qualifications needed. He had to be a believer. The word *adelphos* in verse 3 indicates one with a life based on a common origin, one of one heart and one mind with the apostles. The Scripture says they should be men and does not use the generic term here but the Greek word *andras*, which means male and is also translated "husband" in the Scripture. This office was assigned to males as evident in the wording and the naming of these first deacons. They also had to be men of integrity, "of good reputation." And they were to be "filled with the Holy Spirit" as well as "full of wisdom."

- **The deacon's integration (vv. 3b–4)**

  The pastors and the deacons made for an effective integration of ministry. The deacons were to "serve tables." The word we translate here is *diakonos*. Twenty times in the New Testament it is translated "minister" or "servant." Three times it is translated "deacon." Our concept of the foot washer comes from the root of this word. The deacon's primary task was serving and meeting the physical needs of the members.

- **The deacon's inspiration (vv. 5–7)**

  The coming together of the pastors and the deacons in this biblical way inspires many things. It inspires unity. "It pleased the whole multitude." It inspires the spreading of the gospel. "The word of God spread, and the number of the disciples multiplied greatly in Jerusalem." This generally follows unity in the family of faith. It inspired the pastors to give themselves to their priority, "prayer and the ministry of the word."

When the local church, particularly in the Western world, rediscovers the reason for the ministry of the deacon, as well as the type of men who should serve this office, the ministry of selfless and sacrificial service the office entails and the inspiration it brings, then and perhaps only then can it be said of us what was said of them: "Then the word of God spread, and the number of the disciples multiplied greatly in Jerusalem, and a great many of the priests were obedient to the faith" (Acts 6:7).

PersonalPoints

_____

_____

_____

_____

_____

_____

_____

_____

_____

_____

_____

_____

_____

_____

_____

_____

_____

_____

_____

PersonalPoints

_____

_____

_____

_____

_____

_____

_____

_____

_____

_____

_____

_____

_____

_____

_____

_____

_____

_____

13

The Pastor and His Pastoral Ministry

PowerPoints

Across the years I have observed that there is nothing, outside of the pastor leading his people to Christ, that binds the pastor's and the people's hearts together like weddings, funerals, and baby dedications. As years of pastoral ministry turn into decades, there are weddings, funerals, and dedications that most of us in ministry do not remember. But I guarantee you people never forget who officiated at their wedding ceremonies, who preached the funerals of their loved ones and brought comfort to them in times of need, or who dedicated their babies to God at the church's altar. When performed in love and in the spirit of a servant's heart, the pastor's pastoral ministry in these three specific areas endears him to his people forever and provides his best opportunity of being Christ's hand extended to the people under his pastoral care.

Weddings and funerals are like bookends of emotion for the pastor. Many a pastor has had to go from the hurt and sorrow of ministering to one family at the time of a loved one's death straight to the church to perform a wedding where he is immediately thrust into the joy and celebration of another family's festivities. Perhaps this is why our Lord's first miracle was at a wedding in Cana where he was the life of the party (John 2:1–11), and his last miracle was at a funeral in Bethany where he "wept" (John 11:35) at the grave of Lazarus. Any pastor who senses a call from God to a particular place and who genuinely loves his people will live with this range of emotions. There are times of great joy and rejoicing and times of great sorrow and heartbreak. The pastor is the one who stands with his people and walks with them on the mountaintops and also in the valleys. He weeps when they weep and laughs when they laugh. He provides help and hope to those who hurt.

The pastoral ministry that the pastor performs with his people is one of the things that legitimizes his ministry and binds his heart to the hearts of the people God has given him. In this chapter, the practical nature of the wedding, funeral, and baby dedication will be discussed and then some of the pastoral pressures that come with each of them.

PracticalPoints

The wedding

It is inconceivable that the pastor would perform a wedding without adequate counsel with the couple who is to be married. In my premarital counseling sessions, I have sought to make a point of counseling the couple in three areas—their love, their life relations, and the Lord. That is, I want to lead them to know there are three types of love. There is the love of a physical attraction. There is the love of fondness for each other. And then there is the highest level of love: God's love. Unless the couple knows God and can love each other with that sacrificial, selfless love, they will never know love in its fullest expression.

Life relationships are also valuable. I am speaking here of very practical matters such as who is going to manage the checkbook and pay the household bills. Coming to an understanding of many practical matters before the wedding eliminates a lot of potential misunderstandings after the honeymoon.

Finally, the couple's relationship with the Lord is the most important element of the pastor's counsel to couples who are contemplating marriage. I readily admit that I am not a professional counselor, and often I referred couples to those with special gifts and expertise. It is also helpful for the church to have a multiweek premarital class. Some churches refer to it as The Nearly-wed Class or Before We Say I Do. These classes cover valuable and vital information for the couple planning marriage such as in-law relations, finance, communication, conflict resolution, sex in marriage, oneness, spiritual life together, fulfilling each other's needs, and love as the basis for a healthy marriage. Materials for these types of classes are readily available from Christian bookstores.

As to the actual format of the wedding, the pastor who must serve in the double role of pastor and wedding director might find it helpful to remember a few helpful hints. After the lighting of the candles, the parents are to be seated (always remember that the bride's mother is to be the last one of the parents to enter and the first one to exit). After a selection of special music, the pastor enters first to begin the processional. He is usually followed in by the groom and groomsmen taking their places at the altar. Then the bridesmaids and the maid of honor enter, followed finally by the bride on the arm of her father.

The following is the order and message I used at the wedding of our own daughter, Wendy, to Brian Hermes. Once the wedding party was in place and the bride had been "given away" to the bridegroom, the ceremony continued as such:

"As we begin, I want to thank you, Brian and Wendy, for allowing me the joy of sharing in this evening and also to say thank you to all our family and friends who have gathered here to share in this time of worship with us. We want to thank you not simply for your presence, but for your prayers through the years. And thank you, Brian and Wendy, for bringing to this altar a sense of confidence that God is in this. It is important to me and your mom to be this close to something we consider so good and so godly.

"Wendy, it is special for Susie and me to see how God has honored all our prayers and all our cares through the years: every act of discipline, every moment of concern, every embrace of love and forgiveness. Our joy is so great this evening we have no words to adequately express it. I am very proud to be your dad.

"Mike and Susan [parents of the groom], we want to thank you for the product of your love, this young man who stands at this wedding altar with such character, conviction, commitment, and courage. You have done well.

"Brian, we have watched you grow like Christ in 'wisdom, stature, favor with God and favor with man.' By honoring your parents, you have received God's blessing.

"Susie [my wife], I salute you this evening. You have not only trained Wendy in the way she should go, you have walked that path with consistent example before her across all these years. Thank you for being 'one' with me in such a way that we come here this evening with no real regrets. You have beautifully created in your daughter a model of love that will now be shared with the man of her dreams.

"Brian and Wendy, as you stand at your wedding altar this evening, there are several ways in which you should look: there is the backward look to realize that there have been a lot of people who have made deposits and investments in your lives across the years for whom we are grateful. There is the upward look to realize that God brought you together. We give thanks to him this evening and welcome him to our wedding just as they did in Cana centuries ago. There is the inward look to realize it is not enough to build your life on a love that is carnal, but a love that is Christlike. Finally, there is a forward look to realize that your lives together are to show others a picture of Christ and his church. This very wedding altar is a picture of our own salvation. You, Brian, represent the bridegroom, our Lord Jesus Christ. Just as you entered this room a moment ago to receive your bride, so will he one day come again to receive us unto himself. You, Wendy, represent the bride of Christ, the church. He loves us with a never-ending love and longs to see us return that love in commitment of our lives to him as you are doing to Brian this evening.

"I know that both of you realize the seriousness of this occasion; how that God himself performed the first wedding ceremony back in the garden of Eden when he took a rib from man and formed the woman and one of the sweetest verses in the Bible says, 'He brought her to the man' and they became one flesh (Gen. 2:22).

"You have chosen to come publicly to this altar this evening in front of family, friends, and the Father himself to affirm the leading of God in your lives and the establishment of your home on the principles he has set forth in His word. [At this point I read portions of such Scripture passages as Ephesians 5:22–33 and 1 Corinthians 13:4–8.]

"Now, Brian and Wendy, because of your choice of each other, join right hands and repeat these vows one to another beginning with you, Brian. 'Wendy, because I believe God has brought us together, I take you to be my wedded wife. I promise to love and cherish you, to stand by you in sickness as well as health, good times as well as bad times, times of joy as well as times of sorrow, forsaking all others for you as long as we both shall live.' [This is repeated phrase by phrase and followed by Wendy's similar pledge to Brian.]

"These rings that you have brought to this wedding altar will serve as constant reminders of your commitment to each other. They are valuable, made of gold, which should remind you daily of the value of the home founded on the principles of the Word of God. They are never-ending circles that shall remind you of God's intention of your lives to be never-ending together as long as you both shall live. Brian, as you place this ring on Wendy's finger, I am going to ask you to promise God in your heart you will keep the vows you have made tonight forever. And as you place this ring on her finger, I am going to ask you to make this pledge to her: 'Wendy, wherever you go I will go, wherever you lodge I will lodge, your people will be my people and your God will be my God.' [This is repeated in phrases and then followed by the bride's similar ring pledge to the groom]."

At this point in the ceremony the unity candle is lit and the pastoral prayer is offered as the bride and groom kneel at the wedding altar. After the prayer, the service concludes with the following pronouncement:

"Now, Brian and Wendy, because of your choice in each other and because of the power invested in me as a minister of the gospel, I now pronounce you husband and wife, and what God has joined together, let no one put asunder. [The groom kisses his bride.]

"I now present to you all Mr. and Mrs. Brian Hermes."

[The recessional begins.]

The funeral

There are few times that afford the pastor to be looked upon as Christ's hand extended to his people more than those times of sorrow that surround the death of a loved one. The pastor's mere presence with the people is often more important than anything he might say. He represents the Lord in such a holy moment. As it relates to the death of a church member, let me offer the following helpful suggestions. First, be prompt. Get to the bereaved one's side as quickly as possible. You do not have to stay long, but your simple prompt presence will speak volumes and offer comfort in time of need. Also, be personal. This is not a time for formality but an opportunity to "touch" your people in a very personal sort of way. Weep with your people when they are weeping. Don't shy away from speaking of how much the departed one meant to you personally, and remind the loved ones that they cannot really lose someone when they know where they are. By all means, be prayerful. It should go without saying that the pastor should pray with the family on such sorrowful occasions. And he should leave them with the comfort of a passage of Scripture. On such occasions, I often remind them of the words of the psalmist in Psalm 57:1, "Be merciful to me, O God, be merciful to me! For my soul trusts in You; and in the shadow of Your wings I will make my refuge, until these calamities have passed by."

There will be occasions when the pastor preaches the funeral of one who may not have been a believer. I have often found it helpful to preach a message on the adequacy of God at such times with the following outline: (1) God is adequate for our feelings. He is adequate to comfort us. At this point I use passages such as John 11:35; 14:1–6; and Psalm 23 to illustrate that God is a God of comfort in time of need. (2) God is adequate for our friends in the Lord who go on before us. I am careful here to speak in third-person terms if I do not know the deceased well or have confidence of his or her salvation. Here I speak of heaven and the hope it holds for all those who have put their faith in the Lord Jesus Christ.

(3) God is adequate for our future. We may be saying, "What will I do? I have lost my wife, husband, dad, mom, friend, or whomever." Here I seek to direct people to the hope that God is adequate for tomorrow. Often I will use 1 Corinthians 15:58 at this point: "Therefore, my beloved brethren, be steadfast, immovable, always abounding in the work of the Lord, knowing that your labor is not in vain in the Lord." God is adequate for our feelings, our friends, and our future. Great is his faithfulness.

There will also be occasions of preaching funerals of those good and godly saints in the church who are well-known for their Christlike lives and who are paragons of faithfulness to all who know them. One such man was Ned King, a longtime deacon in Dallas and a dear friend. For more than fifty years Ned and his wife, Edith Marie, were in the heart of everything at our First Baptist Church. At Ned's funeral, I likened him to Barnabas in the early church with the following message: First Baptist Church has had her James, the statesman leader of the Jerusalem church. He was the great pragmatist and prayer warrior who presided with wisdom at the Jerusalem conference of Acts 15. Our James was George W. Truett. We also had our Paul, the educated PhD, and the hot-hearted, fearless preacher-theologian-pastor. His name was W. A. Criswell. We have had a multitude of our Stephens, those faithful deacons across the years who were filled with wisdom and the Holy Spirit. First Baptist has had its share of Philips, those evangelists and missionaries who have gone out to the ends of the earth. Dorcas has also been well represented in our church in the likes of so many women who served faithfully "full of good works." And we can't forget our Lydias, business-women whom God has used in mighty ways. But today we come to remember the man who was our Barnabas. Ned King was the greatest encourager our church has ever known. It is said of Barnabas, "When he came and had seen the grace of God, he was glad, and encouraged them all that with purpose of heart they should continue with the Lord. For he [Barnabas] was a good man, full of the Holy Spirit and of faith. And a great many people were added to the Lord" (Acts 11:23–24). I was captured by that phrase—"He was a good man." Ned King, like Barnabas, was a good man and verse 23 says three things about him. (1) Ned's life was a life of grace. He saw the grace of God. That is what Ned always saw. While others might look with judgment or condemnation, Ned looked with grace. (2) Ned's life was a life of gladness. Like Barnabas, Ned saw the grace of God "and he was glad." He was a happy and helpful man who found his greatest joy in lifting others up. (3) Ned's life was a life of goodness. Like Barnabas, "he encouraged them all with purpose of heart." Ned left us a legacy: he saw the grace of God. He was glad and encouraged us all!

There are many other practical ways to go about the funeral service. If at all possible, the pastor should make the funeral service personal. I have often used an outline that speaks of the person's faith, faithfulness, family, friends, and future. With this simple outline the pastor can address saving faith, faithfulness in life, the love of family, the importance of friends, and the future and hope of heaven to all who know Christ.

Once the funeral proceeds to the graveside, there are some practical matters of which the pastor should be aware. Above all, the pastor should be as brief as possible. I usually seek to remind the people that we do not leave their loved one there, we leave simply the house the Lord gave him or her to live in while on earth. I remind them of this truth for the believer: "to be absent from the body and to be present with the Lord" (2 Cor. 5:8). I also state something to the effect that "yesterday, we read in the newspaper that _____ was dead. But don't you believe it. He is more alive today than he ever was because Jesus said, 'I am the resurrection and the life. He who believes in Me, though he may die, he shall live. And whoever lives and believes in Me shall never die. Do you believe this?'" (John 11:25-26). End the committal service with a prayer, a word of hope, as you dismiss the people back to their cars and to their homes and back to the business of living their own lives, reminded that heaven has been made sweeter for walking this way today.

There is one final word regarding the funeral. Pastor, do not fail to follow up with the family after the funeral. Within the next immediate days, at least one more visit should be made to the home. I cannot express how important this simple act of kindness and concern will be to the bereaved family. Your presence and prayers will help seal the experience in their hearts and will ensure their love and commitment to you and the church. I also found it helpful to write a personal Christmas letter to every family who lost a loved one during the year. The first Christmas without their loved one is often a very emotional one to say the least. In the letter, which reminded them I was thinking of them and praying for them, I enclosed the poem below. On many occasions and after many years, I would find those people with that poem in the flyleaves of their Bibles. I encourage you to print it out for yourself and use it at Christmas. It is as follows:

I've had my first Christmas in Heaven:

> A glorious, wonderful day!
> I stood with saints of the ages,
> Who found Christ, the Truth and the Way.
> I sang with the Heavenly choir:
> Just think! I, who longed so to sing!
> And oh, what celestial music
> We brought to our Saviour and King!
> We sang the glad songs of redemption.
> How Jesus to Bethlehem came,
> And how they called His Name Jesus,

That all might be saved through His Name.
We sang once again with the angels,
The song that they sang that blest morn,
When shepherds first heard the glad story
That Jesus, the Saviour, was born.
O, how I wish you had been there:
No Christmas on earth could compare
With all the rapture and glory
We witnessed in Heaven so fair.
You know how I always loved Christmas:
It seemed such a wonderful day.
With all of my loved ones around me:
The children so happy and gay.
Yes, now I can see why I loved it:
And oh, what joy it will be
When you and my loved ones are with me,
To share in the glories I see.
So Dear Ones on earth, here's my greeting:
Look up till the day dawn appears,
And oh, what a Christmas awaits us,
Beyond all our partings and tears!
—*Dr. Albert Simpson Reitz*

The baby dedication

It is the pastor's joy to share in the happy occasion of the birth of a baby by dedicating the parents to the upbringing of the child "in the training and admonition of the Lord" (Eph. 6:4). Practically speaking, I would have the parents come to the altar with their newborn.

Then I would remind the people that "they brought little children to Him, that he might touch them ... and He took them up in His arms, laid His hands on them, and blessed them" (Mark 10:13–16). I would at this point remind the people that Jesus was the "same yesterday, today and forever" (Heb. 13:8) and that if Jesus were with us physically, he would take the child in his own arms and bless him or her. Since we, the church, are Jesus' visible body in the world today, we, in his stead, take this child in our arms and into our hearts and bless her or him in Jesus' name. At this point I would take the child from the parents, speak a word of Scripture, and kneel with the parents in a pastoral prayer directed at their responsibility to raise the child in such a manner that it will be easy for the child to embrace Christ at the age of accountability. There are many and various verses I personally use in dedication services of parents and babies. Among them: 1 Samuel 1:27-28; Psalm 61:5; Proverbs 22:6; Jeremiah 1:5; Luke 2:52; 18:15-19.

PressurePoints

Weddings, funerals, and baby dedications afford the pastor wonderful opportunities to present the gospel message to individuals who might not necessarily be attending our regular worship services. However, like other aspects of ministry, these events are fraught with certain pressures that the wise pastor recognizes and seeks to avoid.

One will not be in the pastorate long until he is confronted with the pressure of marrying couples who may not be Christians or who may have been divorced. What is the pastor to do in such circumstances? These are often among the most difficult, and potentially most misunderstood, decisions the pastor must make in his pastoral ministry. As a general rule, it has been my practice not to marry couples unless they are both believers and can testify to a born-again experience. To do otherwise should be the rare exception, if at all, and not the rule. For me the Scripture is clear on this subject. As to the divorce issue, it has always been my personal persuasion that this, too, should be done in rare exceptions and not become the rule for the pastor. Many pastors see the exception clause in Matthew 5:32 as freeing the innocent party in a divorce to remarry due to the infidelity and adultery of the departing spouse. But this is never God's desire for any of us to use this verse as an easy way out of a marriage. I know many marriages that have been restored after cases of infidelity and today present beautiful testimonies of the grace of God. A second marriage might be better than a first one, but it can never be as good as the first one could have been. The pastor must prayerfully seek the mind of Christ at the point of these pressures and find a consistency in the way he carries out his pastoral ministry roles.

The pastor will also feel pressure at the point of the funeral. If the pastor is uncertain of the person's salvation, he should avoid at all costs the temptation to "preach a lost man into heaven." There will be many people at the funeral who knew the man and knew his ways. If the preacher places the departed one in heaven, then it gives a false hope of eternal life for all the listeners, many of whom, most likely, need to be converted themselves. The pastor should be caring but honest and present the gospel in some form at the funeral service. I have often felt the pressure of loved ones who feared their lost loved one was unsaved and wanted some kind of assurance from me that God would receive him or her into heaven. I would often quote to them the passage from Genesis 18:25, "Shall not the Judge of all the earth do right?" We must leave all judgment to God who alone searches our hearts and knows our inmost thoughts. Ultimately, we can rest in the truth that God will do what is right.

When we come to the dedication of the baby, we must take caution that the primary issue at hand is the dedication of the parents to the raising of the child with biblical instruction and personal example in the home. Those who may be attending should not be confused with the issue of salvation. I should be clear that in no measure am I affirming or confirming any type of pedo-salvation, but simply coming in gratefulness to God to present the child before the Lord as those did in Scripture and to challenge and pray for the parents to raise their child in such a way that when he or she reaches an age of accountability before God, it will be easier for the person to embrace the claims of Christ upon his or her life and receive Christ as a personal Lord and Savior.

PulpitPoints

What I learned from the wedding

John 2:1–11

Our family has had the happy occasions of seeing both our daughters marry outstanding Christian men. Our first family wedding was that of our firstborn, Wendy, and the young man who won her heart, Brian. The wedding event was the culmination of more than a year of planning and a lifetime of prayers.

In John 2:2 the Bible records, "Jesus and his disciples were invited to the wedding." Many of Jesus' modern-day disciples were invited to Wendy's wedding—they came from former pastorates in Oklahoma and Florida and our present place of service at the time in Texas. And the Lord Jesus attended our wedding just as he did the one in Cana. We were honored by his presence and thankful for his blessing.

As a pastor across the years, I had officiated at hundreds of weddings and given counsel to thousands of people. I had watched so many of my friends move through the same emotions I was feeling on that wedding evening. In the aftermath of it all, I learned four valuable lessons that emerged not only from the wedding in Cana, but the wedding in Dallas as well. Let's look at them and learn from them.

- **Lesson no. 1: The Lord Jesus is with us in our joys as well as our sorrows.**

  So often we only think of Jesus drawing near in time of need, heartache, or sorrow as he did with Mary and Martha when Lazarus was sick unto death. But the good news is Jesus is with us in our joys as well. It is no coincidence that our Lord's first public miracle took place at a wedding, a joyous occasion. His first miracle was not performed in a leper colony or at a funeral, but at a wedding party. It is okay to have fun. He is with us. Jesus was socially connected in his world. The one who had visited the wedding in Cana came to our wedding, and it was his presence that made it a joyful occasion.

- **Lesson no. 2: Life is about relationships.**

  When all is said and done, life is about relationships. It is about our relationship with the Lord and our relationships with one another. Family and friends flocked to Dallas from all over to share with us in that time of celebration. Each of them seemed to share in our joys as though they were their very own. The bottom line is that people matter. They mattered much to Jesus, and they should matter to us as his followers. Life is about relationships.

- **Lesson no. 3: Moms make things happen.**

  While Christ appointed men to places of leadership in the church and in the home, it is the women who really make things happen. Look at Mary. She took over at the wedding of Cana. She takes the initiative (v. 3). She makes things happen (v. 5). She did what most moms do. When she found out there was a need, she took it to Jesus. On the week of our wedding if I heard Wendy call out "Mom!" once, I heard it a thousand times. Moms seem to have inner resources that we dads don't have. They stay up with the kids at night when they are sick. They drive endless car pools. They fulfill crazy schedules, and somehow they get it all done by Christmas. Like Mary, moms make it happen. And her advice in Cana is still good advice today: "Whatever He says to you, do it" (John 2:5).

- **Lesson no. 4: The best is yet to be.**

  I am happy the Lord showed up at our wedding, but I am thankful, as a Baptist preacher, that he didn't turn our wedding punch into wine! That could have caused a few problems for me with some of our more stuffy and legalistic adherents. The common custom of the first century was to serve the best wine first. By the way, this was the common drink of Jesus' day. It was a diluted form of wine, mixed with water. When Jesus turned the water into wine, it was wonderful. The guests recognized it as the best of the evening. The best was saved for last. This is the way it is with Christ; the best is always yet to be in his economy.

I learned a lot from my daughter's wedding. How wonderful that the Lord is with us in our joys as well as our sorrows. Life is truly about relationships. Yes, I readily admit, moms make things happen. And with the Lord the best is yet to be. Mary's advice is still applicable today: "Whatever He says to you, do it!"

PersonalPoints

PersonalPoints

_____

_____

_____

_____

_____

_____

_____

_____

_____

_____

_____

_____

_____

_____

_____

_____

_____

_____

_____

PersonalPoints

14

The Pastor and His Pastoral Care

PowerPoints

Many times in the New Testament we read of the pastor being likened to a shepherd. It is not simply the shepherd's responsibility to lead and feed the flock, but also to care for each sheep in the fold, even that one who goes astray. Only the pastor who has a definite call to ministry from God and who is anointed for the task can have the passion and patience to care for his people.

Paul challenged the pastors at Ephesus to "take heed to yourselves and to all the flock, among which the Holy Spirit has made you overseers, to shepherd the church of God which He purchased with His own blood" (Acts 20:28). Pastor, I challenge you this coming Sunday to look into the faces and hearts of your people and allow this thought to burn in your own heart. These are the sheep of his pasture "which He purchased with His own blood." He is the Great Shepherd and, wonder of wonders, he has assigned and appointed you as his under-shepherd. You are a steward of what belongs to the Lord Jesus Christ! When this reality becomes ever present in the mind of the pastor, it will bring the issue of pastoral care to a new level of importance and dignity. It is not simply the pastor's job to preach. It is not simply the pastor's job to administer the ordinances or perform the funerals and weddings. It is not simply the pastor's job to lead the staff and administer the affairs of the church. It is the pastor's solemn and signal duty to care for his people, to "shepherd the church of God which He purchased with His own blood."

It is an awesome thought to me as a pastor that the Lord has ceded a portion of his flock to me. I am to care for these people as a shepherd cares for his flock. I must love the unlovely and the difficult. I must care for those who are faithful and for those who are unfaithful. I must reach out to those who encourage like Barnabas and those who often doubt like Thomas. It falls to the pastor, like the shepherd, to pursue, protect, preserve, and provide for his people with tender pastoral care.

PracticalPoints

The two most obvious places of the ministry of pastoral care are found in pastoral counseling and pastoral visitation. There are those who come to the pastor for counsel, and there are those to whom the pastor goes to comfort. There are several brief points to be made on both these issues.

The first admonition to the pastor and his counseling is to be cautious. The pastor should know his limitations. He cannot be a specialist in everything. There are times that the pastor must recognize when to recommend someone to a professional in the field of biblical counseling. We do this every day in medicine and other fields, and the pastor must be cautious in the advice he gives. He should be a good listener above all else.

The pastor should also be confidential. One would hope this would go without saying, but unfortunately it is a recurring problem with some in their pastoral care. Do not violate this sacred trust. Never take what you hear in the counseling room into the pulpit by way of illustration without the express consent of those with whom you have shared and then only under unusual circumstances of edification. Be confidential. If and when someone should confess a crime, such as child molestation, that is another issue. Then you should seek the wise counsel of those you respect and not hesitate to take this information to the proper authorities if the need calls for such.

Be conciliatory in your approach. The ministry of restoration and reconciliation as noted in the PulpitPoints below should always be your goal as a counselor caring for your people. If someone has taken the time and initiative to come to you seeking counsel, then most likely he or she are looking for someone to give him or her an honest appraisal of his or her sin. Deal with the sin issue and the hope and promises of restoration and reconciliation found in such verses as 1 John 1:9. Remember that for a broken relationship to be restored, there must be a repentant heart on the part of the offending party and a receptive heart on the part of the offended party.

The pastor should also be consistent in the counsel he gives. It is my opinion that the Bible is all sufficient for our faith and practice. This is not to say that professional counselors do not play an important role in the restoration of hearts and even homes. What I am saying is that the pastor should always give counsel that is consistent with the teachings of Scripture and not contrary to them.

Be compassionate. Show your love and concern not just through your words, but through your countenance and even your body language. People are hurting. They are in need of hope and compassion. They are beat up by and large on Monday through Friday out in the world, and they should be able to expect their pastor to have a compassionate heart when they come to talk with him. Love never fails ... and it covers a multitude of sins.

Now, a word about visitation in the context of pastoral care. As a pastor, I always found it beneficial to me and usually a blessing to others when I left the church and showed up on their "turf" whether it was in their homes, at their offices, or even in their hospital rooms. The following are some lessons I have learned along the way.

The pastor should be pointed in his visitation. Those who receive visits from insurance salespeople expect them to talk about insurance. Those who receive visits from financial advisors expect to engage in conversations about finance. The pastor should not simply talk about the weather, the latest political news, or the most recent sports story. He should speak of the Lord and bring hope to those with whom he visits.

Visitation in the realm of pastoral care should also be polite. Good manners and social graces go a long way in pastoral care. The pastor does not have to be pompous, stuffy, stiff, or formal. Be yourself. Be relaxed. And above all, be polite in your visit.

"Be prompt" is good advice for any visit. If you say you are going to be at a certain place at a certain time, then be prompt. For most of us, time is our most valuable commodity. The pastor should also be prompt in the visit itself. Make it relatively short, especially if it is a visit to a patient in a hospital room. Most likely he or she does not feel well and does not look his or her best. Do not linger long in hospital rooms. Be prompt. Give a good and hopeful word, share a passage of Scripture, and offer a pastoral prayer.

Another piece of helpful advice is to be purposeful in your visits to your members. The great and overwhelming purpose of your heart as pastor ought to be to win others to a saving faith in the Lord Jesus Christ. Keep this purpose at the forefront of every pastoral visit and you will be blessed.

Finally, be prayerful. Each pastoral visit, no matter what nature it may take, should be concluded with a prayer from the pastor for his people. This does something special to someone when he or she hears the pastor pray for him or her. Often, the pastor is tempted to leave without praying. Resist this temptation. It is not from God. Pray with and for your people at every opportunity.

PressurePoints

The ministry of pastoral care lends itself to great temptation if the pastor is not on guard and taking heed as Paul warned. Pastor, never let yourself get into a situation where temptation can find a breeding ground. Never counsel a woman by yourself behind closed doors. It is a good policy for the pastor to have an open, glass window on his office door or to counsel with an open door making sure his secretary or someone else is seated in the adjacent room.

The pastor should be very careful with any physical displays of attention or affection, especially with members of the opposite sex. We are living in a time of heightened suspicion for those in the ministry. It should be the pastor's policy to keep his hands off women who come to him for counsel or with whom he deals in the church. There is a very fine line between the spiritual and the sensual, and even holding the hand of a lady when praying for her can lend itself to awkward situations and temptations.

Another place where the pastoral care of the pastor should be manifested is in the care and concern of his pastoral predecessors. If this volume were not already as long as it is, I would have added an additional chapter on "the pastor and his predecessor." I will, however, say a few important words about this potential pressure point.

Most likely, your predecessor had feet of clay just as you do, with his own strengths and weaknesses even though some in the church may only remember how wonderful he was. The pastor should make it his abiding policy to never criticize nor critique his predecessor on any grounds in front of any of his members. Invite him to visit the church. Let him know he is always welcome. If, with honesty, you can "make over him" before your people, do so. His friends will be glad to see him and hear of his present ministry, and they will endear themselves to you for having the security and the sense to treat him with respect and appreciation. Most likely, a part of your own present success is due to the planting and watering he once did on your own church field. Be secure in who you are and whose you are and be open and inviting to those who went before you.

Remember, as pastor of Christ's church, it is your job to maintain the love and unity of the church. And, above all, remember to "take heed to yourselves and to all the flock, among which the Holy Spirit has made you overseers, to shepherd the church of God which He purchased with His own blood" (Acts 20:28). Yes, pastor, yours is an awesome calling. Walk worthily of it as you go about your pastoral care.

PulpitPoints

The ministry of restoration

Galatians 6:1–2

Like natural earthquakes, moral earthquakes don't just happen! They, too, are preceded by secret faults, little cracks in character below the surface that eventually erupt into moral earthquakes. Of all the entities in the world, the church has the greatest opportunity in our culture to be about the ministry of restoration. It is never too late for a new beginning.

What would happen if, through pastoral care, the church started to become known as the place of real restoration, where those who are down could get up, where those who are out could get in? What would happen if the church became a place of confirmation and not a place of condemnation? Men and women with wounded hearts and homes would flock to our places of worship and find hope and healing.

In the letter to the Galatians, the great apostle gives three succinct steps to follow in the ministry of restoration. What are we to do with our fallen friends?

- **We are to hunt them up! (v. 1)**

  Some of us are better at simply writing them off. Or we often wait for the fallen ones to come back to us. But Scripture tells us we are to be the initiators; we are to hunt them up. The church needs to get past the false assumption that the one who has fallen will initiate the restoration. Often, these individuals harbor a sense of guilt and shame that continues to drive them farther from hope and help. It is our task to hunt them up.

- **We are to help them up! (v. 1b)**

  We are to restore (*katartizō*) such a one. This same Greek word is translated in Matthew 4:21 as "mending" nets. It also appears in 1 Corinthians 1:10, speaking of bones that are "perfectly joined together." It is a medical term that carries the connotation of putting a broken bone back in place so that it can be mended and become useful again. Orthopedics do not heal. They simply put broken bones back in alignment. Then God does the healing, and it takes several weeks to heal a broken bone.

  This is the church's job. We cannot heal broken homes and hearts, much less wounded lives. But we can hunt them up and help them up by helping them put things in order so that God can heal their hearts and restore them to usefulness.

- **We are to hold them up! (v. 2)**

  It is not enough to simply hunt them up and help them up; we must also hold them up. In the words of Paul, "bear one another's burdens." Some burdens are too heavy to carry alone. In fact, there are some burdens that are not made to be borne alone. In the family of God, we need one another.

If we are going to reach our world, we need to realize it is made up of men and women who are hurting and broken. We, the church, are the ones who are called upon to take the initiative in restoration. We are to hunt them up, help them up, and then hold them up until they have found a new beginning.

There is a larger picture at play here. You were the one who was "overtaken in a trespass" (Gal. 6:1). What did the Lord Jesus do with you? Did he wait for you to come crawling back in shame and guilt so he could say, "I told you so"? No. What did he do? He hunted you up. He said, "The Son of Man has come to seek and to save that which was lost" (Luke 19:10). Then Jesus helped you up. He "restored" you to himself. And he continues to hold you up. It is never too late for a new beginning.

PersonalPoints

_____

_____

_____

_____

_____

_____

_____

_____

_____

_____

_____

_____

_____

_____

_____

_____

_____

_____

PersonalPoints

_____

_____

_____

_____

_____

_____

_____

_____

_____

_____

_____

_____

_____

_____

_____

_____

_____

_____

_____

15

The Pastor and His Partner

PowerPoints

The pastor and his partner is not just a catchy alliterative cliché. The pastor and his wife are truly partners in life and in ministry. I like the way the Today's Living Bible paraphrases 1 Peter 3:7b, "Remember that you and your wife are partners in receiving God's blessings." The pastor in ministry whose partner in ministry is one with him is blessed indeed. The pastor and his wife share their sorrows together; they face their problems together; they rejoice in their blessings together. They recognize that "if one can chase a thousand, two can chase ten thousand." A synergistic dynamic takes place when the pastor and his wife are together in the pastoring of the church, in the ministry they have received from the Lord, and in the raising of their children in the admonition of the Lord.

I am blessed and honored to be able to say that beyond question the best and most loyal friend I have had in life is my wife, Susie. The tragedy in many homes is that the husband and wife are not truly friends with each other. They do not share things in common as friends do. They do not communicate with each other as friends do. Vital to the pastor's success is having a true partner in ministry as a wife. Pastor, make sure your wife is your best friend. Let us hear our wives say to us what Solomon heard his wife say to him, "This is my beloved and this is my friend" (Song 5:16).

The wife and family are uniquely the husband's responsibility. If the pastor loses his family, he loses along with it much of the ministry he has received from Christ. One of the primary responsibilities the husband owes his wife is that of being the provider. When Susie and I stood at our marriage altar, she took my name. Think about that. She left the name of her own birth and took from then on the name of my birth! Our children bear my name. This fact puts a tremendous responsibility upon me as a husband. It is my biblical responsibility to be the provider of the family's needs.

We who are husbands have another important task. That is, being the protector of our wives and children. This is certainly true when it comes to the church environment in which the pastor's family lives and has its being. The pastor must protect his wife not simply physically, but spiritually, socially, and emotionally as well. You are her "priest." You have the single privilege of coming to God on behalf of your family. In all the busyness of the modern pastorate, the pastor must remember his main ministry is to his wife, his "partner in receiving God's blessings."

PracticalPoints

Apart from his own relationship with the Lord, there is no relationship more important to the pastor than that of his partner, his wife. The main responsibility in the home lies at his feet. We men often like to repeat the biblical adage "Wives, submit." But in reality, the most important command in the passage on the husband-wife relationship is the one that says "Husbands, love."

We who are husbands have a mandate from God. It is "Husbands, love your wives." The Greeks are much more expressive in their language than we with our English vernacular. We have one word for love. We use this same word to say we love our Lord, or our wives and kids, or our dog, or even certain foods.

There are three words for love in the language of the Greeks. One is *agapē*. This is the love that is best defined by saying no matter what someone may do to you by insult or injury, you will seek only their highest good. This is God's love. This is selfless and sacrificial love. This is the word used in John 3:16 and in the husband's command above to love his wife in Ephesians 5:25.

When the Greeks said "I love you," they often used another word, *philēō*. This is the type of love that carries with it a fondness. It is a liking kind of love. It is a brotherly kind of fondness and affection that we share with our best friends.

Although not found in the New Testament, the Greeks had another word for love, *eros*. We get our word *erotic* from this word. This is the love that wants something for itself. It is self-centered, self-seeking, and fleshly. Most all adulterous affairs are built on this type of love. That is why they seldom last. This is the lowest level of love. It is merely a physical attraction.

The pastor and his wife should have a little of all three in their relationship with each other. There should be a bit of *eros* in the sense that there should be a physical attraction toward each other. A married couple ought to also be able to use the verb form of *agapē* when they say "I love you." There should be that fondness, that liking kind of love, which finds its evidence in best friends. But it all should be built and based on *agapē*, God's love. The most practical thing a pastor can do for his partner is to love her with this selfless love that can only be found through a relationship with Christ himself.

The pastor should also seek to put in practice the method by which he is commanded to love his wife. How? "As Christ also loved the church" (Eph. 5:25). Here we find the single most incredible act of sacrificial love ever witnessed, and it is with this love and in this way that the pastor is called upon to love his wife. He is to love her selflessly. How did Christ love the church? "He gave Himself for her." This means we must deny ourselves for our wives. Paul said, "Love does not seek its own" (1 Cor. 13:5). Jesus put aside any selfish desires, and his love for the church was not determined by whether the church deserved it or not.

Not only are we husbands commanded to love our wives selflessly but also sanctifyingly. Christ loved the church and gave himself for the church "that He might sanctify and cleanse her with the washing of water by the word" (Eph. 5:26). To sanctify means to set apart. Our job as husbands is to help make our wives beautiful Christians. We should set them apart, build them up, encourage them, and love them. The pastor who truly loves his wife seeks and strives for her to be sanctified in the eyes of God. He separates her for himself. This is why divorce is so tragic among believers. It perverts the type. Can you imagine the Lord Jesus disavowing the church, leaving the church? No, he loves us selflessly and sanctifyingly. This is the husband's mandate as well.

I should also add that it falls on us to love our wives not just selflessly and sanctifyingly, but supremely. Our aim as husbands should be to use our lives to satisfy her needs. What wife would not submit to that kind of love? I once had a young preacher who was about to get married say to me, "Pastor, I am getting married in a few weeks, and I fear I love her too much." I remembered reading what Dr. Harry Ironside of the Moody Church in Chicago had said in a similar situation, and I replied, "Do you love her as much as Christ loves the church?"

"Well, of course not," he responded quickly. "Well then, you do not love her enough!" Jesus loved the church supremely.

My wife and I are "one flesh." This is a union closer than a parent and a child. When the pastor and his wife understand they are one flesh, they cease thinking of themselves as two but one. In reality, we are not even partners in the marriage, we are one.

Christ calls this love affair between husband and wife a "mystery." The word means a sacred secret, a mystery with a message. After speaking of the husband-wife relationship, Paul says, "This is a great mystery; but I speak concerning Christ and the church" (Eph. 5:32). The pastor's home is to be a picture to the world of Christ and his love for his church as we love our wives "as Christ loved the church." This is a life commitment. It is forever!

The pastor must love, cherish, and protect his partner in life and ministry—just as Christ loves us and gave himself for us.

PressurePoints

Perhaps there is no more difficult position anywhere than that of the pastors' wives. Her plight is unique and peculiar. It is one of the highest callings one can have, and yet there are thousands of unhappy and discontented pastors' wives today. Many of them live as though they were in a fishbowl or a glass house where their business becomes everybody's business. They often feel the need to please everyone while sharing their husbands with scores, perhaps hundreds, of others. The pastor's home is his most important ministry. If he loses it, he loses much of everything else.

There are several pressure points the wise pastor realizes and thus seeks to eliminate them as best he can. Spending quality time with each other is not only important, it is imperative. And I don't mean visiting the hospitals together. It doesn't have to be large segments of time. I have found great pleasure in simply going for evening walks with my wife. There, the phone does not ring, and there are no interruptions. If at all possible, the pastor should plan a few short trips away with only his wife. It is often just as important to play together as to pray together.

The thing that diffuses pressure as much as anything else is giving spiritual direction to the family. This is among your wife's most important and longed-for needs. Some pastors expend so much spiritual energy at the church and in ministry that there is not much left when it comes to home. Nothing you can do to meet your wife's need is more important than being the spiritual leader of your wife and children. Do not leave that task to her.

We pastors are so busy giving encouragement to others in discovering their own spiritual gifts or abilities that we often fail to be an encouragement in this vein to those who love us most. Build up your wife. Encourage her in the Lord. Challenge her to exercise the gifts of love and service with which Christ has equipped her. She needs constant encouragement from you as her lover … and pastor.

Protect her. I am speaking here from the church. She does not have to be at every meeting. She does not have to be there every time the doors are open. Help her determine what commitments are priorities and what are not. She bears so many of your burdens of which you are most likely not even aware.

Pastor, help your wife understand that if you are called to ministry, then she is too. You are one. She is your true partner in life and ministry.

PulpitPoints

The Bible blueprint for a happy home

Ephesians 5:22–33

The home is the laboratory of life. If we are to have a revival in our land, it must begin with a revival in our homes. The world has a difficult time listening to men and women who try to tell them how to solve all the world's problems when they cannot even solve their own personal problems and their homes are in havoc. In Ephesians 5 is found the real cutting edge in the laboratory of life: the home.

It is no coincidence that these verses related to the husband-wife relationship immediately follow Ephesians 5:21 with its admonition of mutual submission. In fact, that which follows verse 21 is an exposition of the importance of submission in the husband-wife relationship, but also submission in the employer-employee relationship, as well as the parent-child relationship.

Part of the problem in the home today is that some wives have forgotten their roles, and many husbands have forgotten their responsibilities. Let's look at the Bible blueprint for the happy home.

- **The wife's role: a submissive lifestyle (vv. 22–24)**

  Here there is a mandate. Although the word is not found in verse 22 in the Greek text, it refers to the word in verse 21. The word *submit* means "to place under the authority of another." A lot of people would like to take their scissors and cut this verse out of the Bible. It flies in the face of the modern feminist movement. But it is not a dirty word. Paul is not saying "Wives, obey." He says, "Wives, submit."

  He also gives us the method. How is the wife to do this? "As unto the Lord." It has more to do with spiritual attitude than anything else.

  The Bible also speaks of the motive here. "The husband is the head of the wife—even as Christ is the head of the church." The Bible says, "The head of every man is Christ, the head of woman is man, and the head of Christ is God" (1 Cor. 11:3). This has nothing to do with inferiority. God the Father and God the Son are equal to each other as are the husband and wife.

We also find here our model. "And he is the savior of the body. Therefore just as the church is subject unto Christ, so let the wives be to their own husbands in everything."

- **The husband's responsibility: a sacrificial love (vv. 25–33)**

Note the husband's mandate. "Husbands love." That is it. Love! And the word here is *agapē*, that is, God's love unconditional and unselfish. Some marriages are in trouble because the husband tries to be the lord instead of the lover.

Paul also gives us the method by which the husband is to love his wife. "As Christ loved the church and gave Himself for her." How? Selflessly, sanctifyingly, satisfyingly, and supremely. Wives can submit to that type of love because it has their highest needs and concerns in mind.

Finally, we come to the mystery. "This is a great mystery; but I speak concerning Christ and the church. Nevertheless let each one of you in particular so love his own wife as himself; and let the wife see that she respects her husband." Our homes are to be a picture of Christ and the church before a hurting world.

The main responsibility in the home resides with the husband. The one thing upon which he must focus in his relationship with his wife is love. The Bible states that our relationship to Christ himself is as that of a wife to her husband. He loves us selflessly, sanctifyingly, satisfyingly, and supremely. It is easy to respond to love like that.

PersonalPoints

PersonalPoints

_____

_____

_____

_____

_____

_____

_____

_____

_____

_____

_____

_____

_____

_____

_____

_____

_____

_____

PersonalPoints

16

The Pastor and His Parenting

PowerPoints

"There goes the preacher's kid." So often those words are voiced with a note of sarcasm, or they are uttered with some semblance of derision. I do not know of a preacher who ever set out to intentionally neglect his children. However, there have been far too many of us who have "lost our kids" while we were busy taking care of the needs of others. From the first time I read the words of Solomon, in the Song of Songs 1:6, I have been haunted by them and made it my express purpose, to the best of my ability, to see that they were not able to be said of me. He said, "They made me the keeper of the vineyards; but my own vineyard I have not kept." Those are haunting words for any pastor.

The pastor should consider his children at the top of the list of his most important ministries. Our children have a basic need of affection that can be found only through loving parents. This should be spelled l-o-v-e. They also have a need of acceptance. This is best spelled f-o-r-g-i-v-e. They also have a big need of attention that can only be spelled t-i-m-e. Affection, acceptance, and attention are three things every pastor should give his kids. And I am one who believes that the quantity of time is important but not nearly as much as quality time.

My wife and I have been blessed with two daughters, Wendy and Holly. They are both grown now, married, and have children of their own. They have made their mom and dad look so good by the wise decisions in life they have made. Wendy and her husband, Brian, are both attorneys and are active in their church where they teach a Bible study and where he serves as a deacon. Holly and her husband, David, are active in their church where he serves on staff and is an ordained minister. Each day of their lives they have made me proud to be their father, and they are my greatest ministry. I count this as an undeserved blessing. I have other friends in ministry, who I am sure were better dads than I, and yet whose children, for whatever reason, made wrong choices in life. In this chapter, I want to emphasize some of the things that the pastor needs to do in a practical sense in order to make a proper investment in his child's life and then point to some pressures that come to the parsonage when it is the laboratory of life in the raising of a preacher's kids.

PracticalPoints

Parenthood is one institution that cannot afford to talk about its "rights" but must give attention to its "responsibilities." As a parent, I always felt I had three primary responsibilities that I owed my two daughters. I owed my kids proper conduct, positive correction, and personal counsel.

My first obligation to my children was that of my own proper conduct. It falls to me as a father to make sure I do not "provoke my children to wrath" (Eph. 6:4). My conduct should not irritate them or cause them to be resentful. Pastors owe their children a personal conduct that is consistent. Our lives need to match our lips. What we say in the pulpit needs to translate to how we act at home. Children are often provoked when we have one set of rules of conduct for ourselves and one set for them. Be consistent with your child. Your rule should be never to tell them twice to do the same thing. The dad whose conduct is not consistent himself will find it hard to measure out effective discipline. Our conduct also should be compassionate. It should be practiced in an environment of love. And by the way, the Scripture tells us that one of the ways our children will know we love them is through proper discipline. "For whom the Lord loves, he chastens" (Heb. 12:6). The wisdom of Proverbs reminds us that "He who spares his rod hates his son, but he who loves him disciplines him promptly" (Prov. 13:24). At the same time, our conduct should be constrained. Children are to be loved, not provoked. We must be on guard as parents that we do not overcorrect our children. Discipline should never be handed out by an angry parent. One of the most important things the pastor/father can give his children is his own proper conduct that is consistent, compassionate, and constrained.

I also felt as a father that another important part of my obligation to Wendy and Holly was that of positive correction. The Bible admonishes me as a parent to "nurture" my children (Eph. 6:4 KJV). The word *nurture* means to discipline, to teach, to train, to instruct. I have no right to use discipline on my children unless I use positive correction, unless I nurture them in the Lord. The Bible says, "Foolishness is bound up in the heart of a child; the rod of correction will drive it far from him" (Prov. 22:15). Obviously, we are not talking here about child abuse, about beating our children. But we do owe our children not only our proper conduct but also positive correction as well. If we do not correct and discipline our kids, who is going to do so? The pastor does his children a great disservice when he leaves all the discipline to his wife. It is the father's obligation to his child.

We also owe our children the obligation of personal counsel. We are to "admonish them" (Eph. 6:4). This means we are to give them verbal instruction with a view to correct. As parents, it is our job to teach our children to obey. We owe them this personal counsel. Why? Because they will not get it on their own. We do not have to teach them to disobey. They were born with this nature. We all pick it up by our inherent sin nature. Every child of a pastor has the right for his or her dad to give personal counsel. Some pastors give counsel to everyone else and neglect their own children. I always felt the need to make sure that my children had my personal counsel at every stage of life. One of the prayers I prayed regularly for my children was that "the God of our Lord Jesus Christ, the Father of glory, may give to you the spirit of wisdom and revelation in the knowledge of Him, the eyes of your understanding being enlightened; that you may know what is the hope of His calling" (Eph. 1:17–18).

Pastor, give your child the gift of your proper conduct. Be consistent. Make sure what they see and hear in the pulpit on Sunday is the same person they live with through the week. This is what will bring respect for you in their eyes. Give your child the gift of your positive correction. I emphasize the word *positive* here. Love them enough to discipline them and correct them. And by all means, make sure you give them your personal counsel. They are going to get counsel somewhere. Make sure it comes from you.

PressurePoints

No home stands at risk and is in as much danger with being adversely influenced by being oversaturated with religion than the pastor's home. Many a PK (preacher's kid) has been turned off to the church and has remained that way into his or her adult years. This can be brought about by many causes. Some children have borne the brunt and pain of seeing their pastor-fathers berated and humiliated by self-serving and downright mean laypeople in church business meetings. Unfortunately, others have rejected the church in later years because of the lack of integrity and character in their own parents, who posed to be something on Sunday and were completely different behind the closed doors of the parsonage. Pastors' children are pretty savvy when it comes to spotting a phony. The pastor must give constant watch to his own honesty and must show his children he is the same in the home that he is in the church.

As I type these words, my mind is racing back across the years to the early days of our marriage before Susie and I had children. I was speaking at a Bible conference and we went to dinner with the pastor and his family. We went to a particular food establishment where you could order either a regular dinner or one that was billed as all you can eat. To our astonishment, this pastor instructed his children to order the regular, less expensive meal, and he would get the all-you-can-eat special, and then if they wanted more, he would pass it on to them when he asked for more. Sure enough, when the kids wanted more, the pastor asked for a refill of his own plate, and when the waiter left and was no longer looking, he passed it over to his children. I often wondered what effect such behavior ultimately had upon those children. There is no greater gift a dad can give his kids than the gift of honesty and integrity.

Some pastors and their families have been successful in having "family altars" with their children each evening. I must confess we did not do this in our home. Our children grew up in the days when our church in Fort Lauderdale was being unusually blessed of God. On Monday evenings I did not get home from evangelism training and visitation until the children were already in bed. On Tuesday I often had deacons' meetings or the like. Wednesdays brought the regular Wednesday night church routine. And so on. My wife did an incredible job of reproducing herself in the life of our daughters, and I am sure the girls cannot recall a night when they pillowed their heads to sleep without the prayers of their mother hovering over them. Since I stayed in my study at home on most mornings, we found that breakfast time afforded our family the best opportunity to be together. I felt as a father it was more important what I was when I prayed than even what I prayed for my children.

I made sure my children knew what I was praying for them. From their first conscious thoughts, they knew their dad was praying for their purity. Specifically, every time I prayed for them I prayed they would be pure in morals, in mind, and in motives. I let them know this, and I am sure in their teenage years when they would get to temptation's corner, they thought about this.

It is not always easy being a preacher's kid. And it is not easy for pastors to be fathers. Often we are the objects of unfair criticism and ungodly opposition in the church. This can embitter the pastor and cause him to harbor deep resentment in his heart. The pastor should never let his children hear him criticizing or condemning people of the church. Too many kids have been lost to the church because they got in the car with their pastor/father after church and listened to him berate and blame certain church members all the way home. This is one pressure the pastor must resist in protecting his children from many of the hurts that come his way.

Our daughters can tell you that they do not remember a day growing up in our home when they did not hear their father say "I am proud to be your dad." Oh, we had our tensions, misunderstandings, and family quarrels just as everyone else does, but I made it a point to learn to say "I am sorry" when the need arose. Being their protector and provider and having them know I was proud of them every day of their lives have gone a long way in building the character and grace that they bestow today. And even though I am older now and they are grown, I am still very proud to be their dad!

Pastor, love your children. Know when to release them and let them go. Know when to receive them back and even restore them when need be. They are your crown and most important ministry. May you never have to say with Solomon, "They made me the keeper of the vineyards, but my own vineyard I have not kept" (Song 1:6).

PulpitPoints

The model father

Luke 15:11–32

Dads go through all sorts of different stages in their journeys through parenthood. Someone has observed that at age four, our children say, "My dad can do anything." At age seven, they say, "My dad knows an awful lot." At age twelve, they say, "Oh well, I shouldn't expect dad to know everything." At age fourteen, many of them have progressed to say, "My dad is hopelessly out-of-date and old-fashioned." By age twenty-one, they are saying, "What should I expect? He just doesn't understand." At age twenty-five, they say, "Dad knows a little bit more than I might have thought." Then, around age thirty, they begin to say, "I need to find out what Dad thinks." By age forty, they are asking, "What would Dad have thought?" At age fifty, they say, "My dad knew everything." Then, at age sixty, they lament, "I wish I could talk it over with Dad just one more time."

Tucked away in our Lord's most familiar parable is a father. He seems to leave center stage to his two sons, one a prodigal and the other in self-pity. But this parable is really about the father. It begins, "A certain man had two sons." As we look at him and learn from him, we can see much about our own roles as parents.

- **See him with an open hand saying "I release you" (vv. 11–13)**

  This dad was wise enough to know that the way to keep his children was to open his hand and let them go. Many fathers have lost their kids because they gripped them so tightly they never let them go on their own. He could have refused his son's request. He could have held back the inheritance. He could have used blackmail with the money or played the comparison game with the older brother. But here was a dad who was prepared to stand by what he had put in that boy from childhood (Prov. 22:6). Some parents hold so tightly they lose their children. This dad was wise enough to open his hand and let him go. There are always some prodigals who choose to learn the hard way.

- **See him with open arms saying "I receive you" (vv. 20–24)**

  When the boy came home, the father saw him when he was "a great way off," and he ran to meet him with open arms. The boy came walking, but the dad came running! His love had been big enough to release him with open hands; now it was big enough to receive him with open arms. We are not talking here about a boy who came home with the same rebellious spirit, simply sorry he got caught, but here is a boy truly repentant. And here is a dad with open arms.

- **See him with an open heart saying "I restore you" (vv. 25–32)**

  I suppose the most notable characteristic of this model father was his presence and transparency. He was there for his sons no matter what their problems. The most valuable gift he gave them was his presence. When the celebration was on, where was Dad? We find him outside with an open heart assuring the wounded older brother of his love and support.

We need more fathers like this one, a father with an open hand, wise enough to know that the way to lose our kids is to hold too tightly and the way to keep them is to let them go when the time comes. We need more dads with open arms, always ready to make a way for new beginnings. Finally, we need dads with open hearts who are transparent and encouraging.

The real message in this story is that our Heavenly Father deals with us in this same way. He has open hands toward us. We are not puppets but people, and the love we can voluntarily return to him is indescribably valuable to him. He meets us with open arms, and never were they opened as wide as on the cross. He shows us his open heart. He opened it on Calvary for the whole world to see, and he invites us into his arms today.

PersonalPoints

_____

_____

_____

_____

_____

_____

_____

_____

_____

_____

_____

_____

_____

_____

_____

_____

_____

_____

PersonalPoints

17

The Pastor and His Priorities

PowerPoints

The productive and proficient pastor will make sure his priorities are well defined and in proper order. It is a difficult task to seek to bring order and direction into the lives of those who are in the church if they do not see it first modeled in the life of their pastor. It has become a well-worn cliché to say the pastor's priorities should be his relationship with his Lord, followed by his relationship with his wife and family, followed by his relationships and responsibilities with the church. But it is as true today as it was the first time someone wrote down these top three priorities in that order.

The pastor's first priority is to be found in his own private life. This is the part of his life that is hidden from the church and even his family. It is spent alone with God in the secret place. Here he takes in daily from the Word and the Spirit in order to be able to give out in his duties to his family and his church. The wise and effective man of God gives priority to his own relationship with Christ and meets him daily in the place of prayer, devotion, and Bible study. For me, that time has always been in the early morning hours. My mind is not cluttered with the issues of the day and is fresh to hear from God. In my own devotional time, I have found great strength, comfort, and direction from repeating the grand hymns of the faith back to God. I have always believed it was as important what I was as a parent and pastor as it was what I said or did. Being comes before doing because what the pastor does is determined by who he is and what position he has in Christ.

Next on the priority list of the pastor is his personal life. By this, I primarily am speaking of his relationship with his wife and children in the area of those intimate interpersonal relationships that exist behind the closed doors of the parsonage. It is a wise pastor who gives his wife priority over his church. She, along with his children, are his greatest ministry, and unless this number two position is well defined and lived out, the pastor's effectiveness in ministry will never be what it could and should be.

The pastor's private life and personal life are then followed by his professional life on the ladder of priorities. This is his ministry to the church to which he is called and to the people whom he is to shepherd. The reason for this order is not to be found in some well-worn, well-used cliché. The reality is that I cannot love my wife "as Christ loved the church and gave himself for her" unless my priority is to love him supremely. The more I am in love with Christ and becoming like him, the more I can love her selflessly and sacrificially with *agapē*, God's love. And I have always seen the truth that I could never lead my church as pastor if I did not, first, love Christ with all my heart and, second, be in a loving and supportive relationship with my wife.

Priorities are essential in the life of the pastor. James reminds us that "a double-minded man" is unstable in all his ways (James 1:8). Think of how many times we read one thing in the Scripture. "This one thing I do ... one thing you lack ... one thing I know ... one thing I have desired of the Lord." The secret to success in the pastor's life is, in a word, priority. The hardest workers are not always the most productive. The most productive are those who have defined their priorities in the pastorate and hold to them. Number one—the private life. Number two—the personal life. Number three—the professional life.

PracticalPoints

Keep your private life secret.

When we lived in Fort Lauderdale, we had a large grapefruit tree in our backyard. It produced the largest, most delectable and juicy grapefruits one could find outside of Jericho or Jaffa. Most people who ate from it had the idea that the worth of that grapefruit tree was in its public life. It was beautiful as it spread over the yard and its branches bent from the loads of large grapefruits that hung from them. But the real secret of that tree was in its hidden life, its root system that went deep into the earth and brought not only stability against the gale-force hurricane winds that often came our way but also brought the much needed nutrients and water into the trunk, up through the branches, and into the fruit itself. It was that part of the tree that was hidden from view, its secret life, which made the tree as productive as it was. And so it is with the pastor. His private life, alone with God, is his highest priority. He should keep it secret. The public life of the pastor's life and ministry will, over time, prove that it rests on the private life of his own "root system," which should dig deep into the riches of the word of God and into communion with the Father that comes through the Lord Jesus in the power and instruction of the Holy Spirit. Keep your private life secret. It is between you and God.

Keep your personal life separate.

There is something healthy about the pastor who has a part of his life with his family that is separate from the church and its various ministries. There is no question that in the normal traffic pattern of the pastor's life that the church and its activities will consume the majority of his family's time (and, I might add, this is the way it should be), but the wise pastor has an outlet away from the church. I always found it helpful to get away somewhere with my wife for a day or two every few weeks. We made much of vacations when our children were little. In fact, we took them to places that stretched our budget to the limit on more than one occasion, but I always looked at it as if I was buying them a memory. To this day our daughters still talk and laugh about those long car trips we made together when they were young. We found it to be a tremendous bonding time for the family.

Susie and I also have always made it a point to develop friendships and relationships that were outside the church. More often than not, they turned into tremendous evangelistic opportunities. I always found it refreshing to hear the perspective of "outsiders" to the faith as I built relationships with others. In Fort Lauderdale we became friends our first week there with an Italian couple who owned a small restaurant near our home. A friendship developed that eventually ended in seeing this Italian Catholic household come to faith in Christ and be baptized in our church. Pastor, have a personal life that is separate from the church. It will give you perspective on ministry and keep your sanity.

Keep your professional life sensible.

The pastor's work is never done. There is always a little more studying to do; there is always another letter to be written or someone else that should be visited. The pastor could work fourteen hours a day and his task would not be completed. I came to realize that prioritizing my workweek helped to get things done that needed to be done. To this day I carry a note card in my shirt pocket with the week's priority list written down in order of priority. In this way I make sure I get done each day what needs to be done, and some of the peripheral things that are not essential often have to wait for another day. Be sensible. Everyone who needs a pastoral visit may not be able to get one on a given day. Make good use of the telephone. As a pastor, it was not uncommon for me to make fifteen or twenty calls a day to people who needed a touch from their pastor. Most people are wise enough to know that the pastor cannot be everywhere all the time. A simple phone call expressing your concern and interest and a short prayer with them on the phone can work wonders. Be sensible in your pastorate. Prioritize those things like your own Bible study, prayer, sermon preparation, visitation, administration, counseling, staff relations, and the like.

Keep your private life secret. Keep your personal life separate. Keep your professional life sensible.

PressurePoints

Obviously, there will be constant pressure upon the pastor to get these three priorities out of order. It may come from the family, it often comes from the church, and, unfortunately, it sometimes comes from the lack of discipline and even slothfulness of some pastors themselves. Perhaps the greatest pressure comes in the pastor putting the church ahead of his family, in the order of priorities. This is often done in a very nonintentional and even nonobservant way. It has a way of creeping in, and the pastor must be on constant guard at this point. I once asked my pastoral predecessor at Dallas, W. A. Criswell, what he might do differently if he had another opportunity to live his years of the pastorate over again. Without hesitation and with tears welling in his eyes, he said he would have spent more time with his wife and daughter. This warning for all pastors comes from one who had no peer in preaching and pastoral ministry in the twentieth century. It can happen to any of us. Keep your family before your professional duties.

There is also the pressure to put your family or church duties in front of your own devotional and spiritual life. More than one of us has seen this happen and some of us with tragic consequences. We must, as pastors, remember that it is "daily bread." *Daily* is the operative word here. Above all, the busy pastor must guard his private life and keep it secret. The busier we see our Lord becoming in the Gospels, the more he retreated to the secret place to be alone with the Father. We see him ministering to thousands in Galilee and then we immediately see him going up onto the mountain alone to pray. If he who never sinned saw this need of keeping his own priorities in order, how much more do we? Being busy and consumed in ministry is no excuse to avoid keeping our priorities in order. The busier I became as a pastor, the more I saw it as a warning signal to check up on my private and personal life priorities.

This tension that the pastor feels in keeping priorities in line will never go away. It is an issue that must be dealt with intentionally every single day of his life and ministry. Pastor, keep your private life secret, keep your personal life separate, and keep your professional life sensible.

PulpitPoints

Focus

Philippians 3:13–14

Focus is fundamental to pastoral success, or success in any endeavor for that matter. There are so many demands upon the pastor today that there is a tremendous danger to lose focus. When this happens, the main thing is no longer the main thing and simply takes its place among a multitude of things. One of the real keys to success in life is in the ability to obtain and maintain focus. Focus, in fact, will lead you to do four things.

- **Put your priorities in order.**

  Paul said, "This one thing I do ...." Not ten things, nor five things, nor even two things, but "this one thing I do." Focus puts our priorities in order. First, you define your goal, and then it begins to define you.

- **Have a forward look.**

  Focus will cause you to look ahead. Paul goes on to say he was "reaching forward to those things before" him. Paul's focus led him to have a wise forgetfulness about the past and enabled him to make sure his reach continued to exceed his grasp.

- **Go the second mile.**

  Focus brings a passion to the work. Paul said, "I press." The word *press* has with it the idea of an intense endeavor; it is like a hunter who is pursuing his prey. Paul was pressing because he had focus; he had "one thing" as a priority in his life.

- **Know where you are going.**

  One of the most valuable things focus will do for us is to give us a sense of where we are headed. Paul said he was pressing "toward the goal for the prize." The word *goal* translates the Greek word *skopos* from which we get our English word *scope*. Like the scope on a rifle, focus will enable us to get our goals and priorities "in the crosshairs." It enables us to know where we are going and how we are going to get there.

Focus is foundational to successful living. It helps us to begin our task with the end in mind. What is your goal? Can you put it in a sentence? Focus: it will put your priorities in order, give you a forward look in life, lead you to go the second mile, and it will empower you to know where you are going.

PersonalPoints

PersonalPoints

18

The Pastor and His Personal Life

PowerPoints

Being comes before doing because what we eventually end up doing is most always determined by who we really are. Being does not eliminate doing; it accelerates it. In the pastor's personal life, it is as important, if not more so, what he "is" when he preaches and ministers than what he actually says and does. People would rather "see" a sermon in the life of their pastor than "hear" one any day. The gospel according to you is your most powerful and productive message. Our examples are always much clearer than our words. The pastor must take special care that his own personal life is beyond reproach and that his character is spotless.

The words of the psalmist Asaph regarding King David are very poignant at this point. He noted that David "shepherded [his people] according to the integrity of his heart, and guided them by the skillfulness of his hands" (Ps. 78:72). These two attributes, integrity and skillfulness, should be the model and goal of every pastor who is assigned to shepherd a flock of God's own people. The pastor should have integrity in his personal life, and he should strive for excellence (skillfulness) in all that he does. It is a tragic truth that many pastors have lost their influence and platform due to a lack of integrity in their personal lives.

PracticalPoints

What is the most important element in the pastor's ability to lead his people? Some think it is intellect. After all, knowledge is power we are told. This idea indicates that if the pastor simply knows more than others, it enables him to lead effectively. Another says that the most important element in the pastor's effectiveness is intensity. This is the passion that comes with the pastorate, the ability to dream dreams and cast visions with dynamic intensity about the task. Still others believe it is insight. This is the keen ability to discern and see into circumstances and situations with wisdom and insight. While all these are important to the pastor and his leadership, they are not the most important element for him to possess. Pastor, make no mistake about it, integrity is your most valuable asset as you shepherd your people. Your personal life and the integrity you show go farther than anything else in endearing your people to follow your leadership.

Over the years I have watched hundreds of pastors. I am thinking now of a man I knew who had an incredible intellect. He was versed in the biblical languages. He could speak intelligently on virtually any subject from ministry to mythology, from theology to philosophy. But he had little integrity, and he is no longer in ministry today. I have known others who had intensity about their task. They had unbelievable skills in influencing their audiences and getting people motivated for ministry. However, they had little integrity, and it caught up with them and they have taken their place as castaways, as Paul had feared about himself. Then I can remember those with keen insight who could decipher a situation in a moment but who, unfortunately, did not have integrity to go along with it, and they are doing something else today and are no longer in ministry. Pastor, your integrity in your personal life is your most valuable commodity. Live your personal life in such a way that it might be said of you what was said of King David that you "shepherded your people with the integrity of your heart and the skillfulness of your hands" (see Ps. 78:71–72).

Personally, I have found that few things have been as beneficial to my own personal life as having a mature older mentor, and at the same time having a younger pastor whom I was mentoring myself. These two disciplines on either side of your personal life will keep you accountable and on the cutting edge of ministry. Be a Timothy to some older, wiser, experienced pastor. This need not take a lot of time. You may simply have someone you have lunch with from time to time or can call and discuss issues. Then find someone to whom you can be a Paul. Give counsel and support to younger men. You will find this investment of your time will do more for you than anyone else. This is one of the ways integrity in the ministry has been passed down through the years from generation to generation.

PressurePoints

Pressure in the personal life comes in forgetting where this integrity is to be rooted in our lives. The pastor lives in four different and distinct worlds. He has a private life. No one enters the realm of the pastor's private life. Not even his wife knows all his innermost thoughts. No one lives in the pastor's private life—except him and the Lord God who "searches our hearts and knows our innermost thoughts."

The pastor lives in another world, which we might call his personal world. Here he lives with a handful of people who truly know him as he really is; that is, in the intimate world of close interpersonal relationships. In this world he lives with his wife and children and perhaps one or two close friends in life with whom he is intimately acquainted.

Then, of course, the pastor lives in the world of his professional life. Here he interacts with dozens, or scores, or for some, hundreds of individuals as he performs his duties as pastor to the people. These people do not know him personally in the realm of those close relationships, much less privately, but they do come into contact with him in what could be defined as his professional world.

Finally, the pastor has a public life. Some people call it his public persona. This is the world in which he lives that when people hear his name, they have an opinion of him one way or another. Now they may not know him in a professional setting, much less a personal or private one, but they do know who he is in the community and they usually have an opinion about him.

This brings us to the question of where our integrity is rooted. Some must believe it is rooted in our public life because they do all they can do to "spin" their image before the public in a myriad of ways. But integrity is not rooted there. It is only revealed there as to whether we have it or not. Pastor, if you are living a life that lacks integrity, you will be found out. God will either expose it before the world or take away his hand of anointing and blessing from you. Your integrity, or lack thereof, will eventually be revealed in the public world either for God's glory or for your shame.

There are those who seem to believe that integrity is rooted in the professional world: on the anvil of practical experience where we beat out these principles of integrity in front of those with whom we work and minister. But it is not rooted there; it is only reinforced there. If we have integrity, it will be reinforced by what we do and how we do it as we go about our work and ministry.

Thus, someone suggests integrity must then be rooted in our personal life of those close and intimate interpersonal relationships. But it is not rooted there. It is simply reflected there in the pastor's relationship with his wife and children and close friends. If you want to know if I have integrity, ask my wife who has lived with me behind closed doors for more than thirty-five years now. Our integrity is reflected in the lives of those we love around us.

Integrity is rooted in the private life, that world in which we live where only God himself lives with us. The secret life, the hidden life, the life we live with God is where he roots integrity in our hearts. Then note what happens. It begins to be reflected to those in our personal world, reinforced in front of those in our professional world, and, eventually, revealed in our public world for all to see and for all glory to be given to God. Pastor, be a man of integrity. You will never rise above the level of your own personal life in ministry.

Another important issue in the personal life of the pastor is balance. Remember that our Lord grew "in wisdom and stature, and in favor with God and men" (Luke 2:52). Like our Lord, we should give heed to grow intellectually. More attention will be given to this in chapter 23. The pastor should also continue to grow in physical wellness. There is a real stewardship in taking care of yourself physically. Many pastors totally neglect this aspect of their personal lives, and it is to their shame and possibly their own demise. It should go without saying that the pastor should never stop growing spiritually. One of the things I have sought to do all through life is to continue with Scripture memorization. And like Christ, the pastor should also give attention to his social life and grow "in favor with men." He should be winsome in his witness and in his ability to build relationships with those around him. Those early believers had "favor with all the people" (Acts 2:47).

Pastor, pressures will come to tempt you to compromise in your personal life. Learn a lesson from Joseph. He stayed pure because he said no from the very beginning. Be wise enough to do the same and do not begin to flirt with temptations that most surely will come your way. Stay pure in morals. Stay pure in mind. Stay pure in motive. Personal integrity is among your most valuable assets in ministry. Without it, your keenest abilities will become your worst enemies. Make certain your personal life is a clear reflection of everything you preach from the pulpit, and the blessing of the Lord will be upon you.

PulpitPoints

Integrity: Don't leave home without it!

Daniel 6:1–28

What is the single most important trait of one who desires to truly make a difference in our world today?

Some say it is intellect or knowledge that is power. Others point to intensity, a spirit of conquest, a contagious passion for what we do. Still others argue that it is insight, a particular vision that leadership brings that can be adopted by one's peers. However, as noted above, the single most important characteristic of leadership is integrity in the personal life.

Daniel was certainly a man of intellect (Dan. 1:4). He was a person of intensity (Dan. 1:8). He had insight as we readily see in Daniel 2 and Daniel 5. But what truly set him apart and enabled him to achieve such incredible success in Babylon was his integrity (Dan. 6:3).

We, like Daniel, live in the midst of four distinct spheres of life and influence. You have a private life—that part of your existence where no one goes but you and God. You have a personal life—that part of you that is shared by a small circle of family and perhaps a friend or two who knows you intimately. You have a professional life—that part of your world that consists of scores, perhaps hundreds, of individuals with whom you connect weekly at work, at school, or in civic or social activities. Finally, you have a public life—that part of you that is sometimes referred to as your public persona where, when your name is mentioned, people who may have never known you on a professional level, much less a personal or private level, form an opinion about you for good or bad. This brings us to an important question: where is integrity found?

- **Integrity is rooted in your private life (vv. 1–3).**

- **Integrity is reflected in your personal life (vv. 4–5).**

- **Integrity is reinforced in your professional life (vv. 4–10).**

- **Integrity is revealed in your public life (vv. 11–28).**

Integrity is not rooted in the public life. It is only revealed there as to whether we have it or not. Those with little integrity will eventually be exposed publicly. Integrity is not rooted in our professional lives. It is only reinforced there. If we have integrity, it is reinforced in our everyday dealings where we beat out its principles on the anvil of personal experience. Integrity is not even rooted in the personal life of close, intimate relationships. It is only reflected there in our dealings with those who truly know us. Integrity, as beautifully illustrated in the life of Daniel, is rooted in the private life. It is that part of you that will live as long as God lives, the real you in close communion with the Lord himself. When we root our integrity with God alone, then, just as natural as water running downhill, our integrity will be reflected to those in our personal world with whom we love and live, reinforced in our professional world with those with whom we work, and, finally, revealed in the public world for the glory of God.

May it be said of you and me at the end of our journeys what was said of Daniel, and expressed generations before him of King David, that we led our people with the integrity of our hearts and the skillfulness of our hands.

PersonalPoints

_____

_____

_____

_____

_____

_____

_____

_____

_____

_____

_____

_____

_____

_____

_____

_____

_____

_____

PersonalPoints

19

The Pastor and His Possessions

PowerPoints

Possessions. There is nothing inherently wrong with them, unless, of course, those things that we possess begin to possess us in the process. It may be that more pastors have lost their way while bowing at the altar of possessions than at the altar of promiscuity. "Things" have a way of finding their way into our lives and onto the throne of our affection and attention. The pastor must be wise in the stewardship of his possessions.

Our possessions can be of themselves a bit paradoxical. No matter how much we may have, there is always someone who has more. No matter how little we may have, there is always someone who has less. I know people with little means who seem to be more preoccupied with money and possessions than some wealthy people I know. The real issue is not whether we have possessions but whether our possessions have us.

Many people have the attitude that money is all we need to solve our problems whether at the church or in the home. But it seems the more we have, the more we seem to need. The more we make, the more we seem to spend. Far too often a raise in pay simply lends itself to a little more indebtedness. Money is deceptive. If the pastor is not careful, it begins to possess him, instead of him possessing it.

Our money talks. In fact, it speaks volumes about what we think is really important. It is so much a reflection of what lurks inside us that the Lord Jesus spoke often about it. One out of every three of Jesus' parables had to do with money. Thirty-eight of his parables are recorded for posterity and one-third of them dealt with our possessions. He said, "Where your treasure is, there your heart will be also" (Matt. 6:21). Jesus was a diagnostician. He knows that how we deal with our money and our things is a vital reflection of our own spiritual health.

As far-fetched as it may seem, our finances and the way we treat our possessions generally mark the position of our own spiritual pilgrimage. If I was asked to write your biography and could have only one item to use, I would not ask to see your Bible in order to read your marginal notes and underlinings, nor would I ask to see your prayer journal in order to read your daily petitions, nor would I even ask to see your diary. If I could have only one item to write your biography, I would ask to see your checkbook. I would want to know what your canceled check register was saying, for this would tell me what was really important to you in life.

Pastor, always keep in mind that we are nothing more than stewards. Everything we possess will be in someone else's name in a few years. The land we own today was in someone else's name a few years previously. We own nothing. We are simply stewards passing through. We came into this world naked and with nothing, and we will leave it the same way. Keep control of your possessions. Hold them loosely so that they do not control you.

PracticalPoints

I have previously mentioned the name of W. Fred Swank. I do so because this pastor, my father in the ministry, was a man who modeled each and every chapter I have written. He beat out on the anvil of experience these principles in front of all of us in the church. He was a paragon of faithfulness and integrity. I remember well the day he taught me to tithe. I was a college student, just surrendered to the ministry, and was serving on the staff at the church. On a given afternoon he summoned me to his office. Now since he knew my salary and had obviously checked my giving record, he knew I was not tithing. When asked about it, I explained that my pending marriage and college tuition and other responsibilities had prevented it. This found no sympathy with the noble pastor. He took my checkbook and challenged me to make sure every time I deposited my paycheck to make certain the very first check I wrote was to return the tithe and more to the Lord. Being convicted in my own heart about it and fearful that he would be holding me accountable, I began that practice. It has been almost forty years since that day, and I can confess that I have never deposited a dime of income that I did not immediately write a check for a tithe or more to the Lord. It is a discipline I have found that is filled with reward and blessing. It is also a safeguard against allowing my possessions to possess me.

Three important things need to be heeded when we talk of the pastor and possessions. It is important "how we get it, how we guard it, and how we give it."

First, we pastors must take care in how we get it. The pastor needs to take great care and caution in how he gets his possessions. Gifts from individuals often come with all kinds of strings attached to them. Pastor, be wise in this issue. The lure of business deals in and around the church should be handled with extreme caution and wisdom. As I type these words, I remember that it was the love of money that was at the root of Christ's own betrayal. Judas loved money. Yes, this one among the Twelve received thirty pieces of silver, a hefty sum, and look how he got it! Our money talks. Be careful how you get it.

Second, we pastors must also be mindful of how we guard it. How some people guard their money and hoard it up is revealing. Guarded wealth that is not used for Christ promises to bring joy but brings only misery. When we begin to love money and possessions, they cease to bless us and begin to curse us. Some think that just a little more money and just a few more possessions to hoard up will bring happiness, but that is a deception. There is nothing wrong with money, but money that is hoarded will never spread the gospel of Jesus Christ. However, money in the hands of a faithful steward can be a tremendous testimony.

Third, it is also important that we who are pastors remember that how we give it is also vital. Our money talks primarily in the way we give it away. We live in a world today where accumulation is the name of the game. Caught in this trap, many people get all they can and guard it as long as they can. Some of us foolishly must think that the issue at the judgment seat will be "How much have you accumulated?" or "How much have you guarded?" However, the Lord's questions on that day will most likely be "What kind of steward were you? What did you do with what I entrusted with you?" The tithe belongs to the Lord and Scripture says, "It is holy to the LORD" (Lev. 27:30). The tithe is a wonderful place to begin in our stewardship but a faithless place to end. There is a very real sense in which we do not truly give anything until we give above the tithe. Surely, those of us in this dispensation of grace would not desire to give less than the Jews gave during the dispensation of the law. Pastor, be generous. Be a giver. You will honor God and be a blessing to others in the process.

On another practical note, the pastor should make sure he has a will. There are many practical reasons for this. It will ensure that your possessions are distributed as you desire. It prevents a lot of potential misunderstanding among your children and heirs. It will reduce expenses and alleviate taxes, which can in turn leave more of your money to the ministries close to your heart. By the way, there is a reason it is called a last will and testament or testimony. Someday, when you are in heaven, this will be your last opportunity to give testimony to Christ as to what was important to you on this earth. It will be in some lawyer's office, courtroom, or wherever there will be those gathered to hear your final testimony. May it be one that pleases Christ and advances his kingdom on earth even while you are with him in heaven.

PressurePoints

When we come to these stress points, pressure points, in the realm of the pastor and his possessions, we face the issue of debt. Debt can have a detrimental and even devastating effect on the pastor's witness and ministry. If you find yourself in the grip of continuing debt, the very first thing you need to do is stop incurring more debt. You may have to sell something of value. But make a decision to stop getting deeper in debt.

Many pastors I know need to have some plastic surgery. By this, I mean they need to cut up and do away with many of their credit cards. I was fortunate to have a wise pastor who mentored me on this point years ago. The first two years of mine and Susie's marriage, we did not even use a credit card. If we could not pay cash for what we needed, we did without. This discipline got us off to a good start and brought about some habits we have practiced throughout our lives. Since those first two years, we have used credit cards for record keeping purposes, and I am blessed to be able to say we have never gone thirty days without paying them off. For those who can, this is the best policy.

If you are in debt, do not hesitate to immediately talk to your creditors. Assure them of your intention to pay your debt and seek to work out a repayment schedule with them in which you are at least paying something each month. Most people will work with you at this point and be appreciative of your honesty and forthrightness.

Next, consolidate your debts as best you can. Go to your local banker or financial planner and sit down with him or her to seek counsel regarding a consolidation loan. This will make certain you will have only one centralized bill to pay each month and will help along the way to getting debt-free. That is, of course, if you do not continue to assume other debt in the meantime.

I am amazed in talking to pastors at how many of them have never sought to have a family budget, much less tried to live within one. Everyone needs some concept of how and why they should budget their income.

Above all, the pastor should be diligent here in order to maintain his witness and credibility in the community and in the church. Many people speak of the 10/10/80 approach to dealing with possessions. Here we make sure the first 10 percent of our income goes to the Lord knowing that he has a way of making the rest go farther. The tithe is holy unto the Lord. The next 10 percent should go into some type of savings vehicle, and the rest, 80 percent, is what we should seek to live on. While on the surface this seems impossible for some, those who practice it have amazing success.

The pastor and his proper use of his possessions can make or break the ministry he has received from the Lord. Pastor, be careful how you get it, how you guard it, and how you give it.

On another front, the pastor will also find pressure in being asked to support and give to a myriad of worthy things beyond the scope of the local church. Long ago someone shared with me some valuable questions to ask in determining my own giving and stewardship. The first of these is "What is the motive?" Before giving, I seek to understand what it is the particular people are trying to do and why. Another important question is "What is the manner?" Here you should have knowledge of the manner in which they go about what they do. For instance, do the lives of the leadership seem to match the stated purposes of the ministry? A third question is "What is the method?" Is it consistent with the motive?

Do they have integrity? Finally, one should ask, "What is the measure?" What about the results? Are lives being positively impacted for God's glory? I have found that my own personal stewardship and my ability to trust the Lord in giving generally mark the direction of my own spiritual journey.

PulpitPoints

Setting the stewardship standard

Proverbs 3:9–10

Money consumes many of us in our current culture. Our churches are full of bankers, financial planners, stockbrokers, money managers, venture capitalists, CPAs, lawyers, and all kinds of men and women who are constantly giving financial advice. How would you like the free counsel of a man who has been recognized the world over as one of the wealthiest, most successful, and, to top it all off, one of the wisest men who ever lived? This particular gentleman wrote the book on international commerce. His name? Solomon. Listen to his counsel to you and me on money management : "Honor the LORD with your possessions, and with the firstfruits of all your increase; So your barns will be filled with plenty, and your vats will overflow with new wine" (Prov. 3:9–10).

There are a lot of questions regarding stewardship today. How much should I give? How can we possibly afford to return the tenth of our income to God?

However, there are four formidable questions every believer should ask about his or her own stewardship.

- **What is the purpose of my stewardship?**
  "Honor the Lord."

- **What is the product of my stewardship?**
  "With your possessions."

- **What is the priority of my stewardship?**
  "With the firstfruits of all your increase."

- **What is the promise of my stewardship?**
  "So that your barns will be filled."

The greatest stewardship verse in the entire Bible is found in John 3:16: "For God so loved the world that He gave ...." The Lord Jesus was the product of the Father's stewardship to you and me. He was God's only Son, the firstfruit of all of us who would be born again after him. What a privilege is ours to honor the Lord with our own lives and with the firstfruits of our own possessions. He said, "Those who honor Me, I will honor."

PersonalPoints

PersonalPoints

20

The Pastor and His Pressures

PowerPoints

Stress! Perhaps no other word describes the pressure that many pastors are feeling. Webster's Dictionary defines stress as "pressure, intense strain; to bind tight, to subject oneself to external forces." Many pastors reading these words right now are saying, "You are telling Noah about a flood." There is high anxiety in the high calling of ministry.

There is a growing epidemic in the church today of firing the pastor. Even as I write this chapter, I have talked today with a brokenhearted pastor who was terminated without just cause from his church this week. This brokenhearted pastor wept as he poured out his heart and his feelings of desperation. There are all sorts of unique issues with which the pastor feels the pressures of the pastorate. There are some who fall into discouragement and even depression over the perceived lack of response and success in their churches. There are those who are disillusioned by not seeing their dreams come true or their goals met. Some are hurt by the unwelcome and unwarranted criticisms and gossip of people in the church. And then there are those who feel the despair that comes from the apathy and indifference of many in the church who will not get in on what God seems to be doing. There are also those who seek to carry on ministry while being devastated by their own children who have made bad choices in life. And what about finances? So many pastors are living on meager wages, and the financial pressure that comes with trying to meet his family's needs can easily divert his attention from ministry. There is no other position in any other profession that knows the pressure that comes the pastor's way.

One of the things that brings added pressure for those in ministry is the fishbowl effect. In the pastorate, many of us are forced to live our lives in the full view and scrutiny of many of those around us. Our wives and children seem always to be on display. We are expected to be superhuman in many ways. Some churches make demands on pastors that cannot possibly be met. There is high anxiety in the high calling of ministry today.

If one does not think stress is problematic in the pastorate today, simply examine the health insurance programs of the major denominations. For several years the number one and number two medical claims of our Southern Baptist pastors were for musculoskeletal and circulatory issues; that is, such ailments as back problems, high blood pressure, and the like. Both of these issues are defined as preventable diseases. They are most often the result of being overweight or living sedentary lifestyles that can be directly traced to stress and pressure. The top two pharmacy prescriptions are for stress-related issues.

One might assume that the added responsibilities of pastors of larger congregations lend themselves to more stressful and pressure-packed circumstances. Not so. Just the opposite is true. The smaller church pastor has more demands placed upon him. He has the similar demands in sermon preparation but is unable to delegate many of the pastoral and administrative duties and thus is expected to be all things to all people of the church. This brings added stress to the pastor's life.

The unreal expectations placed upon many pastors result in a workaholic mentality. Because of the nature of the pastorate, many of God's servants are less likely to have a close friend and confidant than any other person in the church or community. And all the while, he feels the pressure of trying to be the caregiver to everyone's needs. Most pastors I know are constantly overwhelmed by the preaching and teaching deadlines, and many are surrounded by people with whom it is often difficult to work. Having said all this, it is no wonder stress is among the pastor's major enemies. But stress does not have to be our foe. It can actually be our friend when we learn that we all must live with it and there are ways to deal with it. Let's get practical now and learn to turn it to our advantage.

PracticalPoints

Avoid stress. How many times have we heard that admonition? Our goal is really not to avoid stress. It is inevitable. Stress is a part of our lives. Stress happens. It is not going away. We simply need to put some practical measures in place to learn to deal with it.

Stress can actually be purposeful. The pastor must receive wisdom from God in dealing and coping with the stressful pressures of the pastorate. It is important to keep a sense of humor. The Bible reminds us that a merry heart does us good like medicine. It is also important to take regular time off, to get away from it all. If our Lord sensed a need to retreat by himself as he so often did, how much more do we need to do the same in ministry today? Many pastors I know do not get nearly enough sleep, seldom if ever exercise, and eat unhealthy and unbalanced diets. It is no wonder they become open targets to stressful situations.

Not only should we take care of ourselves physically, but it goes without saying that there is a spiritual dynamic to dealing with stress. It is strange that many of us in ministry fail to pray when we need it most, when we are enduring times of discouragement and stress. The busier our Lord became and the more stressed his circumstance or situation, the more he prayed. He immersed himself in the Word of God. When Jesus was stressed in those classic temptations recorded in Matthew 4, we remember in each instance he used the Word of God in standing against the stressful trials and temptations. Should we not react in kind? In times of pressure, the pastor should be moved to a passionate longing for deeper prayer and more devoted Bible study. Nothing helps overcome the pressures of the pastorate more than getting "a fresh word from God" on which to stand and have our being.

Pressure can be dealt with by any pastor. Begin by remembering that there is a spiritual issue involved. Thank God for your blessings and your burdens. Make a conscious choice to begin to deal with your own well-being. This may mean beginning a systematic exercise program. The body, mind, and spirit are interrelated. Proper nutrition is the source of our energy. Drink at least eight to ten glasses of water a day and eat smaller, more frequent meals that are low in fat content. Stay away from fried foods and too many soft drinks and caffeine. Also, remember that Jesus preached the Sermon on the Mount to show us that our reactions are often more important than our actions. Be careful that you do not respond too quickly in stressful situations with un-Christlike attitudes.

PressurePoints

There are several indicators that will help to identify these stressful pressure points in our lives. There are physical signs. Such things as tension headaches, back pain, change of appetite, change of sleep habits, and higher blood pressure are often warning signs that stress is building within us. There may also be behavioral signs. These could include a loss of productivity, strained relationships, loss of concentration, overeating, compulsive behavior, and the like. Some of the more obvious signs begin to appear in the emotional realm. These usually include things like depression, a loss of a feeling of self-worth, a feeling of failure, frustration, withdrawal, or even isolation. Then, of course, there are spiritual signs such as a loss of the devotional life, a loss of focus and concentration in the prayer life, and a loss of passion and concern for a lost world around us. Ignoring these warning signs most likely will bring trouble in the physical, emotional, mental, and spiritual realm. Wise is the pastor who recognizes his pressure and takes action to deal with it before it deals with him.

PulpitPoints

High calling—high anxiety

James 1:1–12

James addresses his New Testament letter to those who are "scattered" outside of Palestine. He is writing to those early Jewish believers who were under tremendous stress in having to leave their homes, their jobs, their properties, everything they knew during the Diaspora of the first century. He is also writing to twenty-first-century believers who are living and ministering in one of the most stressful times in human history. Our pastors are under tremendous stress in our churches today. Therefore, James begins his letter by pointing out five fascinating facts that can help to turn our stress from our foe to our friend.

- **Stress is predictable (vv. 1–2).**

  James does not say "if" we face these stressful trials, but "when" we face them. Often someone calls upon us to avoid stress. This is impossible in ministry. Stress is predictable. Stress happens. It is going to come our way.

- **Stress is problematic (v. 2).**

  Just because trials and the stress they produce are predictable does not mean that we should treat them lightly. Stress can be problematic as it brings these various trials of which James speaks. Stress is often at the root of so many of our physical problems such as hypertension, high blood pressure, and gastric disorders. Of our thousands of ministers in our health program, the number one and number two medicines prescribed each year are both stress-related drugs.

- **Stress is paradoxical (vv. 2–4).**

  James says we should consider it pure "joy" when we face these stressful trials. We generally count it joy when we avoid trials, not face them. The word James employs here means to think ahead. Job was thinking ahead when he said, "He knows the way that I take; When He has tested me, I shall come forth as gold" (Job 23:10). Job did not consider it a joy in the midst of his stress, but he, like James, looked forward to the joy that would follow his trial.

- **Stress is purposeful (vv. 3–8).**

One purpose of our stressful trials is to lead us to purity (v. 3). Another purpose is to lead us to perseverance (v. 3). Still another is to lead us to perfection (v. 4). The one who never undergoes and learns to stand up under stressful trials will never move to maturity in the Christian life. James reveals it also leads to prayer (v. 5).

- **Stress is profitable (vv. 9–12).**

Someone has said that a Christian is like a tea bag. He is not worth much until he has been through some hot water. Yes, stressful trials can be profitable for the person in poverty (v. 9), the person with plenty (vv. 10–11), and the person with pressure (v. 12).

Stress is predictable. It can be problematic. It is a bit paradoxical. But in the end, it is purposeful and even profitable in the life of the believer. In the words of James, "Blessed is the man who endures temptation; for when he has been approved, he will receive the crown of life" (v. 12).

PersonalPoints

_____

_____

_____

_____

_____

_____

_____

_____

_____

_____

_____

_____

_____

_____

_____

_____

_____

PersonalPoints

21

The Pastor and His Politics

PowerPoints

Perhaps no other aspect of local church ministry demands more wisdom and caution than the pastor and his place in local and national politics. Here in America we have a "government of the people, by the people, and for the people." This very form of government begs the participation of its entire populous. Just because we are "in the church" does not mean we cannot or should not participate in the politics of our country. After all, we pay our taxes, pray for our leaders, are affected by public policy like everyone else, and vote our values. The question comes in what constitutes the right balance for the pastor and politics.

Some tell us the pastor and the church should wash their hands of all political activity. Others continue to challenge us to get immersed in the political process. The pastor must remember that it is not the church's primary responsibility to protest and picket in order to clean up society, but it is the church's task to evangelize the society. The way those first-generation believers turned their world upside down was by changing people's hearts from within and not by seeking to influence society from without. When confronted about his political activities by the Roman governor Pontius Pilate, our Lord replied, "My kingdom is not of this world. If My kingdom were of this world, My servants would fight, so that I should not be delivered to the Jews; but now My kingdom is not from here" (John 18:36). The hot political issue of his day was the Roman occupation of Judea. Jesus did not take sides on the issue and addressed it by saying, "Render therefore to Caesar the things that are Caesar's, and to God the things that are God's" (Matt. 22:21). This does not mean, however, that we are not to be, as He put it, the "salt of the earth" and the "light of the world" (Matt. 5:13–14) in a culture that is decaying and dark.

When issues of moral or ethical concerns arise, they often demand that we hear "a certain sound" from the pastor. Elijah faced King Ahab with boldness and authority when he saw the wickedness of policies and practices were decaying his country. It was Nathan who had the courage on a moral issue to face King David with the words "You are the man." And John the Baptist did not hesitate to stand tall for righteousness in the face of a wicked government even though it cost him his head. And although the Lord Jesus saved his most poignant words and pointed fingers for the religious Pharisees of his day, he did call King Herod a "fox."

The pastor must remember that the power God honors in the church is not political power, but the power of his Holy Spirit in and through his followers. Today's pastor must be certain that he does not find his power in the politics or persuasions of man no matter how right or moral or ethical they may be, but in the power of God alone. How shall the pastor practically deal with the issues of politics from the pulpit, and what pressures should he be careful about as he performs his work of ministry in the local church? Let's examine this question below.

PracticalPoints

I know of no other issue that has been perverted in modern-day pastoring and politics more than the First Amendment to the Constitution, which deals with freedom of religion. Note, it is not freedom *from* religion as so many would have us believe. The First Amendment of the Constitution was intended and written to guarantee the church's freedom of religious expression and not to take it away.

In the Sermon on the Mount, Jesus used two very descriptive metaphors in order to drive home the Christian's duty to his or her society. He declared that we were to be "salt and light" to a world that was decaying and dark (Matt. 5:13–14). Salt serves as a preservative. It does not take a large amount of salt to season a large mass. A little salt in a baked potato can make a huge difference in its taste. Salt preserves and it flavors. Light illumines the darkness. We are to be "salt and light" not in the church, but in the words of our Lord, "You are the salt of the earth;... you are the light of the world." It is out there in the world, in the culture, in society where we are to flavor, preserve, and bring light. This is our duty as believers. We cannot accomplish this by retreating into the confines of the four walls of our churches and being absent from the issues of our society around us. This begs our involvement in the life of community and nation.

There are many practical things the pastor can do that are well within the framework of the law and within the responsibilities of the faith. He should address with biblical instruction all issues with moral or cultural ramifications. He should encourage civic involvement on the part of his people in order to be salt and light where they live. As a pastor, I was always cautious not to invite political candidates to speak at the church for any reason unless all the candidates were invited and allowed to attend. Since Christians have an obligation to vote, it is also commendable to engage in voter registration, provided it is clear the pastor and church are not promoting any one candidate or political party. Along these lines, the distribution of candidate surveys and voting records should be done with caution. The pastor should make certain these types of informational pieces avoid any editorial opinions and that they cover a wide range of topics and are not simply single issue focused.

PressurePoints

There is a danger that comes when the pastor finds himself becoming too overtly immersed in the secular politics of his time. His message is a spiritual one. His mission is an evangelistic one. And yet, his responsibility is also to lead his people to be the salt and light of their society that Christ called upon them to be. There will often be people in the church who will pressure the pastor to do virtually anything and everything to see that a particular candidate is elected. There will be others in the same church who will pressure the pastor to do absolutely nothing to lift a finger in any way that would be perceived to be political. Both of these extremes usually have their own interests and concerns at heart. The pastor must be wise in what he does in this regard and even wiser in how he does it.

The pastor should not endorse publicly from the pulpit any candidate nor should he blatantly oppose for election any candidate. The church should not under any circumstances of which I can conceive contribute money to any political action committee. The pastor should resist the pressure to publish in the church's bulletin or weekly church newsletter any editorial or column that endorses or opposes a particular candidate for public elected office. Nor should he campaign, raise funds, or publicly endorse with the influence of the church any candidate. It is acceptable to pray at rallies or events as long as no official endorsement by the church is apparent.

Because pastors influence such large constituencies of people, they come under increasing pressure from various political parties. This works on both sides of the ecclesiological aisle. Liberal politicians have a long history of speaking from more socially or liberally oriented pulpits during election years. While the more conservative politicians have caught on to this a little late, they have certainly caught up with this and are not timid in seeking to find their place in the more conservative churches as election time draws near. There is even an aggressive attempt to acquire the mailing lists from the church rolls by both political parties. Under no circumstance should the pastor ever betray the confidentiality and trust of his people by giving their names and addresses to any outside group no matter how lofty he might sense their goals to be.

As a pastor, I do not believe my people ever had any doubt about where I stood on any of the moral or ethical issues of the day. With the polarization of the political parties over certain moral issues, this usually lends itself to a perception of identification with a particular political persuasion. The pastor should, to the best of his ability, seek to avoid being identified with any political party. For one thing, politics have a way of embarrassing the overtly active pastor sooner or later or in one way or another. But more important, as a pastor, I never wanted to intentionally ostracize any one segment of my community from hearing the gospel message. After all, the pastor's primary task and calling is to preach the gospel to every person. The wise pastor finds a fine balance in seeking to evangelize the lost and bringing righteous and godly influence upon the political process.

PulpitPoints

America: Some "why" questions

Jeremiah 8:5–22

We should make no mistake about the fact that our nation is becoming morally bankrupt because we live by a philosophy that seldom asks "why" questions and most often simply asks "what" questions. Take almost any issue that plagues our culture. Teenage pregnancy is a good example. Do we ask "Why?" No, we ask "What? What shall we do about it?" So we distribute condoms to our teenagers in public schools. The same logic applies to most issues we face whether they are drugs, AIDS, or whatever. We are asking "What?" when we ought to be asking "Why?"

Jeremiah lived in a day much like ours. His country had been blessed and had prospered but had forgotten her roots and her God. Jeremiah was a man with a burden for the way in which his country had turned its back on God. With a weeping heart, he asks, "Where is the Lord, Who brought us up out of the land of Egypt?" (Jer. 2:6). Then he came straight to the bottom line with a word from God himself, "They have turned their back to Me, and not their face" (Jer. 2:27).

Jeremiah was not into the "what" questions. He asks four hard "why" questions in chapter 8 of his prophecy. These are the same four "why" questions America needs to be asking herself in these days.

- **A question for the American public (v. 5)**

  "Why has this people slid back?"

- **A question for the American pew (v. 14)**

  "Why do we sit still?"

- **A question for the American politician (v. 19)**

  "Why have you provoked me to anger?"

- **A question for the American pulpit (v. 22)**

  "Why is there no recovery? Is there no balm in Gilead? Is there no physician there?"

We are living in the most important days of modern history. These are days of tremendous possibilities. Revivals are usually born out of days of great despair when hope is almost gone. It is not too late—if we stop asking "What?" and begin to deal with root issues by asking "Why?" Don't blame our politicians. We have a generation in America today who does not know Christ because we have failed to make him known. Jeremiah said it best, "Ask for the old paths, where the good way is, And walk in it; then you will find rest for your souls" (Jer. 6:16).

PersonalPoints

PersonalPoints

_____

_____

_____

_____

_____

_____

_____

_____

_____

_____

_____

_____

_____

_____

_____

_____

_____

PersonalPoints

22

The Pastor and His Poor

PowerPoints

Some churches seem to target their ministries toward people they think can help them. They tend to fish for men with a certain type of lure that only one type of fish will bite. New Testament churches were always going after people they could help. They fished for men with nets and, therefore, caught all kinds of people. The pastor's ministry to the poor and rejects of the community will do more to legitimize and energize the church than anything else.

When we look at the life of our Lord, he had a special affinity for the poor. He was born in the most impoverished circumstances imaginable. The King of Kings and the Lord of Lords was not born in a palace, a hospital, a hotel, or even the common decency of a clean room. He came into this world under the most destitute conditions imaginable—a cave filled with animals where sickness, disease, and even death were all likely possibilities. We try to beautify the stable in Bethlehem, but it was in the midst of dung and filth that our Lord entered this world.

Throughout his life Jesus maintained this special relationship with the poor. When Mary and Joseph presented Jesus at his dedication in the temple, they could only afford two turtledoves as a sacrifice. Thirty years later when Jesus stepped out of the carpenter's shop, walked across the dusty streets of Nazareth, and stood up in the synagogue to preach his first sermon, these were his first words: "The Spirit of the Lord is upon Me, because He has anointed Me to preach the gospel to the poor" (Luke 4:18).

Another interesting insight into his relationship with the poor took place when John the Baptist was imprisoned. John sent his own disciples to ask the Lord if he was truly the Messiah or should they keep looking for another. Jesus simply told John's friends to go back and tell their leader that "the poor have the gospel preached to them."

All through His life Jesus maintained this emphasis on the poor. He died in poverty. He was buried in poverty. He had to be placed in a borrowed tomb. Many of his early followers were poor. Peter and John confessed to the lame man at the temple gate, "Silver and gold I do not have, but what I do have I give you" (Acts 3:6).

The first-generation pastors of the early church maintained this affinity toward the poor. In Galatians 2, Paul relates his trip to Jerusalem to meet the pastors there seventeen years after his Damascus Road experience. They concluded that Peter would stay in Jerusalem and preach the gospel to the Jews and that Paul and Barnabas would take the gospel out to the Gentile world.

Upon leaving, Paul relates an incredible happening. He says, "They desired only that we should remember the poor" (Gal. 2:10). Think about that. As he left the mother church to go on his missionary journey, first and foremost on the minds of the leaders in Jerusalem was that Paul would remember the poor and preach the gospel to them.

Many of us in the church today have forgotten the very people around whom Jesus and the early church centered so much of their lives and ministry. There are over four hundred powerful promises in the Bible for those who will take seriously this ministry to the poor.

- **"Blessed is he who considers the poor; the LORD will deliver him in time of trouble. The LORD will preserve him and keep him alive, and he will be blessed on the earth.... The LORD will strengthen him on his bed of illness; You will sustain him on his sickbed" (Ps. 41:1–3).**

  Here is the promise of protection, blessing, and hope for those who remember the poor.

- **"For He shall stand at the right hand of the poor, to save him from those who condemn him" (Ps. 109:31).**

  Where is the Lord Jesus? He is not only at the right hand of the Father; he is at the right hand of the poor. I keep this verse in my mind when I see the poor and seek to be Jesus' hand extended to them.

- **"He who oppresses the poor reproaches his Maker, but he who honors Him has mercy on the needy" (Prov. 14:31).**

  Here is a solemn warning about being a reproach to God! When we show mercy on the poor, we honor the Lord in the process.

- **How about this promise: "He who has pity on the poor lends to the LORD, and He will pay back what he has given" (Prov. 19:17).**

  What a promise! And God pays far better interest and dividends than the local bank or lending institution.

- **"Whoever shuts his ears to the cry of the poor will also cry himself and not be heard" (Prov. 21:13).**

  Some of us wonder why our prayers are unanswered. This could be a part of the reason.

- **"He who gives to the poor will not lack, but he who hides his eyes will have many curses" (Prov. 28:27).**

  Could it be that the reason some churches continually fail to see financial ends meet is because of this supernatural principle of neglecting the poor? The Bible says, "The righteous considers the cause of the poor, but the wicked does not understand such knowledge" (Prov. 29:7). I am convinced we cannot be right with God and continue to have no concern for the poor and keep isolating ourselves from the very kinds of people among whom Jesus spent his entire ministry. The disposals in our church kitchens each Wednesday evening eat better than many of the people in the neighborhood.

Jesus maintains a special affinity to the poor. The pastor who desires the blessing of God for himself and his church will realize this and begin to be Christ's hand extended to these special people. Remember, Jesus stands "at the right hand of the poor."

PracticalPoints

Jesus said, "For you have the poor with you always" (Matt. 26:11). They are all around us, in every city and village. The question is, what are we, the church, going to do about it? Will we take seriously the words of Christ to "remember the poor?" Or will we go on hoping that another federal program will come through? Many federal programs are but indictments on the church for not remembering the poor. Our own Jerusalems are full of people who are hungry, hurting, lonely, defeated, uneducated, and poor.

A new day dawned on our church in Fort Lauderdale when we decided we were intentionally going after the kind of people no other church seemed to want. The words of Jesus pierced our hearts when he said, "When you give a dinner or a supper, do not ask your friends, your brothers, your relatives, nor rich neighbors, lest they also invite you back, and you be repaid. But when you give a feast, invite the poor, the maimed, the lame, the blind. And you will be blessed, because they cannot repay you; for you shall be repaid at the resurrection of the just" (Luke 14:12–14). We acted on those words and began an annual Feast of Plenty. We spread tables across our parking lots and downtown streets for thousands of guests and provided a full-course turkey dinner for them. Hundreds of our people served on various committees, and it has continued for more than twenty-five years. Out of it sprang a myriad of ministries to the poor from literacy classes to clothing rooms, from job training and placement to medical clinics. It is a joy, to this day, to see that feast in downtown Fort Lauderdale. Professional businesspeople and bankers serve for hours washing the filthy feet of street people at the foot-washing booth.

Ministry to the poor will do something for your church. I found the secret to getting our people involved in ministry in the illustration of the good Samaritan. There are four steps to involvement. First, we must see the need. A lot of us see needs but never act on them. Still others drive past a hundred mission opportunities to go to church and talk about missions because we do not see needs all around us. The Samaritan "saw a man" on the highway side beaten and left for dead. Second, we must feel the need. The Bible says, "His heart went out to him." I always felt if I could just get my good and godly people to see needs, then they could begin to feel them. But this is not enough. Third, we must touch the need. The Samaritan leaned over and bandaged the man up. He touched the need. This is the reason we started ministries like the Feast of Plenty. It gave our people a forum to touch needs, and they were never the same again. Finally, we must follow up the need. The Samaritan took the beaten man to the inn and came by later to check on him and pay the bill. Once we have touched a need, it moves and motivates us to follow up and keep ministries to the poor in the forefront. Blessed is the church that takes seriously Christ's command to minister to the poor and puts it into practice practically.

PressurePoints

The church who neglects the poor has robbed itself of a wonderful blessing from God. It seems the pressure point of this subject comes at the point of the ministry to the poor, becoming simply another social program. If we are to be like Jesus, then our primary emphasis will be to take the gospel to the poor. A world of social ministries has sprung up in various churches and organizations that seem to be solely humanitarian and even humanistic in their approach. Our command from the Lord is to take the gospel to the poor.

The temptation is to go out and find the modern-day prodigal son in the pigpen. Then we gather a group together to build a shelter over his head, we go by the clothing closet and put some clothes on his back, and we even take him a hot meal each afternoon. But unfortunately we leave him in the pigpen. Our job is to make sure we give the gospel to the poor. Our real job is to get that boy out of the pigpen and back to the father's house. Interestingly enough, when he gets back there, the Father has a way of meeting his needs "according to His own riches."

The pastor who sets out to minister to the poor and the rejects of society may well find resistance in many churches who are comfortable in their surroundings. However, the more we become like our Lord, the more we will show mercy on the rejects. After all, who led the children of Egypt out of bondage? A social reject, a slave, even a murderer whose name was Moses. Who slew Goliath? A reject named David, a ruddy-faced shepherd boy who was the least son of Jesse of Bethlehem. Who gave us almost half our New Testament? A reject named Paul who was a prisoner in Rome. And who wrote Revelation? A reject. His name was John, and he was exiled to Patmos as a useless old man over ninety years of age.

When Jesus went to Jerusalem, where did he go? He went to the Pool of Bethesda where a large group of impotent people were lying. He went to the poor and rejected. When he went to Jericho, he did not head for city hall to meet the mayor. He went to a blind beggar rattling a tin cup by the side of the road. When he went through Samaria, he did not head to the governor's house. He went to a well in order to meet a reject, and he told her of living water. And when our Lord died, he died between two rejects and took one of them by the hand and into heaven. The more we become like Christ, the more we will intentionally set out to minister to the types of people he spent his entire ministry lifting up.

God in his infinite wisdom and mercy uses the rejects. Jesus loves the rejects and the poor. The only institution in the world that goes door to door seeking a bunch of poverty-stricken people whom the world says will be liabilities instead of assets is the local New Testament church. Pastor, make sure you lead your people to "remember the poor."

PulpitPoints

What about the poor?

Matthew 5:7

The Beatitudes of our Lord do not compose a set of rules by which we are to live, but, instead, present a convincing picture of the life that each of his followers should live. The pathway is plain. First, we are to recognize our abject spiritual poverty. "Blessed are the poor in spirit." We are nothing without Christ. Once this is accomplished, we move to the next beatitude and "mourn" over our spiritual neglect. This brings us to a place of "meekness" or surrender to our Master. Then, and only then, do we begin to "hunger and thirst for righteousness" and be filled. And what is the result of our being controlled by the Spirit of God? The rest of the Beatitudes present the fruit, the proof, the result of coming under the control of our Master. The first evidence is "Blessed are the merciful, for they shall obtain mercy" (Matt. 5:7). Show me a person being controlled by God's Spirit, and I will show you someone who shows mercy to others. On the other hand, show me someone who does not have mercy toward others, and I will show you someone who is not being filled with the Holy Spirit.

What about the poor? In light of the Scriptures, the plight of the poor is a question that no body of believers can avoid. Jesus addressed this subject on a Galilean mountainside in Matthew 5:7 with a pronounced blessing and a promised benefit.

- **A pronounced blessing … "Blessed are the merciful."**

   What does it mean to be merciful? It is not merely some humanistic idea that if we are good to others, they will, in turn, be good to us. Jesus was the most merciful man who ever lived. He reached out to the sick and healed them, he gave new legs to the cripple, he drew the despised tax collectors, prostitutes, and outcasts into his circle of love, and he called the lonely to himself and made them feel loved. He was the most merciful man who ever lived, and yet they screamed for his blood.

When our Lord pronounced this blessing, he was speaking of our relationship to one another. Mercy is seeing a kid at school who is just wishing someone would speak to him and showing that kid some attention. Mercy is seeing someone in need of real love and taking the time to give it. Mercy is seeing the lonely and sharing comfort. Mercy is meeting a need, not simply feeling it.

- **A promised benefit ... "For they shall obtain mercy."**

Do you see this cycle in play? God bestows mercy upon us, then we give mercy to others, and God gives us more mercy. The one who truly receives mercy will be merciful. The one who truly receives forgiveness will be forgiving. The one who truly has received love will be loving. The reason it is so hard for some to forgive is because it has been so long since they have sensed being forgiven.

The eternal truth of Scripture is that we "reap what we sow" (Gal. 6:7). What a pronounced blessing and what a promised benefit we receive from our Lord— "Blessed are the merciful for they shall obtain mercy." In light of the many scriptural admonitions, there is a question every pastor and every church should face: what about the poor?

PersonalPoints

_____

_____

_____

_____

_____

_____

_____

_____

_____

_____

_____

_____

_____

_____

_____

_____

_____

_____

_____

PersonalPoints

23

The Pastor and His Pedagogy

PowerPoints

Pedagogy? This is the art or science of study and teaching. For the pastor, study is a discipline that should never stop. It is one of the constant disciplines that accompanies our calling. It is impossible to be the pastor-teacher we are called to be without the discipline of a consistent, committed, and habitual study life.

Different professions demand the use of various tools of the trade. Carpenters use hammers and saws. Physicians use stethoscopes and thermometers. Plumbers use wrenches. Dentists use drills. The pastor has a particular tool that he must use in order to effectively and efficiently carry out his calling. The pastor's tool is words. The way in which a pastor masters the use of words will largely determine his ability to accomplish his mission in the transferring of his message. Solomon said, "A word fitly spoken is like apples of gold in settings of silver" (Prov. 25:11). Since God has given us language in order to communicate his truth to others, it should naturally follow that the one whose task it is to communicate this sacred truth should study to be skillful and proficient. Pastor, words are the tools of your trade.

Make certain you have a good grasp of English grammar and use your words to communicate gospel truth in such a way that nothing you say takes away from the beauty and truthfulness of God's word.

This is why we are admonished to "be diligent to present yourself approved to God" (2 Tim. 2:15). The pastor's life should be one of continual study no matter whether he is just starting out or whether he is decades along the journey. The pastor never stops learning. The word *study* means to set your heart upon, to be diligent. God's approval is to be your constant concern. Not only should the study of Scriptures be a daily discipline for the pastor, but his passion for his calling should demand his knowledge of church history and contemporary theological issues. To this day, although I am personally years removed from the pastorate, you will find a theology book on my nightstand. Most nights I will read a few pages before turning out the light to go to sleep.

PracticalPoints

There are endless practical points that illustrate the necessity of the pastor's continual discipline of study. I mention only a few below.

Depending on the power and the anointing of the Holy Spirit each time the pastor speaks does not eliminate his need to have a proper working knowledge of the English language or whatever native tongue he uses to communicate the gospel. Pastor, study the language. Learn English grammar. You can do it. Keep building your vocabulary daily no matter how old you might be. Several e-mail sources will send you a new vocabulary word each morning. Remember, words are the pastor's tools of service.

Make a practice of memorizing Scripture. Many pastors have not memorized a new verse of Scripture in months or even years. Scripture memory is a wonderful discipline to not only hide the word in your heart but also to keep your mind sharp as you grow older. I have found it a blessing to memorize the hymns of the faith also. I was converted to Christ as a seventeen-year-old. That particular Sunday morning was the first time I had heard the gospel preached, and the first Christian hymn I sang was "Come, Thou Fount of Every Blessing." I took the hymnal home that day and memorized that song. Only heaven has recorded how many times since then I have come to temptation's corner and those words surfaced in my mind—"Prone to wander, Lord, I feel it. Prone to leave the God I love. Here's my heart, O take and seal it; seal it for Thy courts above. O to grace how great a debtor, daily I'm constrained to be."

Be a prodigious reader. The pastor should read various newspapers, journals, magazines, and articles. The well-read pastor is better informed and more able to illustrate biblical truth to his hearers in a way they can grasp and with which they can identify. The wise pastor will have a grasp of two important topics in his continual discipline of reading. These two topics are church history and theology. Keep a theology book on your nightstand and read a couple of pages each night before you retire. It will keep you thinking and keep you on the cutting edge of contemporary Christian thought. An ongoing knowledge and grasp of church history will prove valuable in deepening your understanding of the lessons learned by those who have gone before us.

Develop your own filing system. Nothing will be as advantageous to you as the years unfold before you if you can have ready access to the voluminous readings and studies you have previously done. None of us can keep in our heads all the pertinent information we have gleaned and gathered over the years. Several systems are available to the busy pastor today to assist in this endeavor. Find one that fits your style, adapt it to your own needs, but whatever you do, have a proper way to file the fruits of your study for future use.

Use your pen. Write notes. Write out your sermons. I have found writing out the full manuscript of my messages not only to be a good discipline, but an effective tool for future study and research. Use words from your pen to encourage and comfort others along the way.

Study Greek. Think about it. Does it make sense that if we have the original language in which God has given us his word that we who are called by him to deliver it would not want to know and understand this language in which it is given? I confess that in the years that ensued after seminary, the busy life of a pastor got in the way of keeping up with a study of Greek. I remember well the day in Fort Lauderdale when I got one of J. Gresham Machen's Greek textbooks and tapes and began a year of daily studying Greek in the privacy of my own study. It opened up a new world to me. Since that time as a pastor, I sought to make it a steady practice to journey through a different Greek text each year to maintain a working knowledge of it. Pastor, "Study to show yourself approved unto God."

PressurePoints

When we speak of the pastor and his pedagogy, his need of a lifestyle of continual study, pressure points often come at two extremes. There are those who get so immersed in the passion of study that they become isolated and secluded from the world around them and hence have little concept of what their people are dealing with in the normal traffic patterns of everyday life and the challenges they bring. On the other hand, there are a few it seems who seek to "wing it" from one pastorate to another with little or no study and a pattern of backslapping and maneuvering their way though life and ministry. The effective pastor is one who seeks the balance of intensely knowing the word of God and intimately knowing his people.

Perhaps the pastor's most persistent pressure point at the point of pedagogy today is the temptation to preach someone else's sermons, even verbatim in some cases, without credit. More than one pastor has lost his platform of ministry because of this. While it is perfectly all right to glean from what others have done, the pastor must guard against this practice, taking away from the discipline of his own word studies and sermon preparation. With the proliferation of sermons on the Internet today, the temptation is great to spend less time digging out the hidden treasures of the gospel from the open pages of our own Bibles. This robs the pastor of passion and the people of the blessing of the pastor's message being conceived, gestated, and born out of his own heart in the secret place with God. It is fine to read other people's sermons, but, in my opinion, it should be the practice of the pastor not to do so until he has done his own study and developed his own outline of the text before him. Remember, Paul said, "For I received from the Lord that which I also delivered to you" (1 Cor. 11:23). He did not say, "For I received from Peter (or James or anyone else) that which I delivered unto you."

PulpitPoints

Study ... to be approved

2 Timothy 2:15

One of the great temptations of the busy pastor who has preached for years is to stop his studying. After all, he has a file of hundreds of previous sermons and is most likely to have changed churches every few years. Not only this, but at his fingertips he now has thousands of sermons available via the various Internet sermon Web sites. Paul admonished Timothy, and us, at this point by saying, "Be diligent to present yourself approved to God, a worker who does not need to be ashamed, rightly dividing the word of truth" (2 Tim. 2:15).

- **The pastor's mandate.**

  "Study." The word means to be diligent, to be zealous about your task and calling. Since reference is made later in the verse to "rightly dividing the word of truth," Paul is challenging the pastor to be zealous with his preparation to preach and his own study habits. The pastorate is one position where study should never end. This is our assignment, our mandate from God.

- **The pastor's motivation.**
What is it that should motivate the pastor to desire to continue studying the Scripture all his days? It is that when he is presented before the Lord Jesus, he might be "approved" by him. Our teaching ministry is a stewardship from God, and the pastor should be motivated by a passionate longing to please his Lord.

- **The pastor's manner.**
What is the manner by which he should go about his task of study? He is to be a "workman who does not need to be ashamed." Study is hard work. Getting out our tools of exegesis and exposition is labor intensive. We are about the "work of the ministry" as Paul mentioned to the Ephesians. The pastor is to be a "workman" who gives himself wholeheartedly to the work of study.

- **The pastor's message.**
All of this is to be done in order to "rightly divide the word of truth" for the people under the pastor's hearing. The pastor is not to take this lightly. He should fear mishandling the word of truth. He should not twist the truth by looking at every paraphrase he might find in order to find a phrase or word that fits his own thinking. We are to rightly divide the word of truth. The pastor has no other

message than that which is centered in and issues out of God's holy Word.

Each of us pastors, as God's workmen, will be either "approved" or "ashamed" when we stand before God. This is the pastor's high calling and awesome task, to "be diligent to present himself approved to God, a workman who does not need to be ashamed, rightly dividing the word of truth."

PersonalPoints

PersonalPoints

_____

_____

_____

_____

_____

_____

_____

_____

_____

_____

_____

_____

_____

_____

_____

_____

_____

_____

PersonalPoints

24

The Pastor and His Pay

PowerPoints

In my experience I have known few pastors who would ever broach the subject of their salaries or related compensation. Traditionally, this seems to always show up on the taboo list. Personally, I have never discussed matters of compensation with any pulpit committee or personnel committee unless it was initiated by them and insisted upon by them. In fact, most pastors I know have turned down raises in salary almost as often as they have received them. But the pastor and his pay is a legitimate item of discussion and one that the local church has a stewardship to address and to address adequately.

Churches are responsible for their pastors and those pastors' families. At GuideStone Financial Resources, it is our sacred responsibility and joy to be not only a steward but also an advocate for scores of thousands of pastors. We are calling upon local churches to take responsibility for their pastors' care. This is not only right; it is biblical. The apostle Paul addressed this very issue in several of his epistles to the church. To the Corinthians he wrote, "The Lord has commanded that those who preach the gospel should live from the gospel" (1 Cor. 9:14). To the

Galatians he admonished to "let him who is taught the word share in all good things with him who teaches" (Gal. 6:6). It is interesting to note the apostle's divinely inspired choice of words in these verses. He says the Lord "commands" this. He also says those who are the recipients of biblical truth must share with the teacher. In one of his final letters, he says to young Timothy, "Let the elders who rule well be counted worthy of double honor, especially those who labor in the word and doctrine" (1 Tim. 5:17). With these words in mind, those in places of leadership in the church should adequately compensate their pastor and his family as he "labors" in the word and doctrine (see appendix A for more about GuideStone's vision and purpose).

The subject of a pastor and his pay is one that should be seriously addressed annually by every church. It should not be left to the pastor to initiate conversation related to his compensation. It is the sacred duty of the church itself. In fact, the Lord "commands" that the church be a good steward in compensating those who minister among the people.

PracticalPoints

One of the great disservices done to the local pastor is for the church to compensate him with a package approach. By this I mean the pastor is paid a lump-sum salary package, and it falls to him to divide it among his car expense, health insurance, retirement contribution, business expenses, and salary. This arrangement forces the pastor to pay considerably more in taxes than he may legally owe. For example, by wisely using the salary and benefits approach rather than the package approach, the church can use tax savings on a $40,000 total package to effectively increase the pastor's cash salary by $2,100 annually, net of taxes, without even giving a monetary raise. Note the example below:

Beyond the approach to the salary package, there are several practical aspects that should be attended to regarding the pastor and his pay. One of the most effective advantages at the pastor's disposal is the housing allowance feature. The pastor can deduct from his salary the lesser of the monthly housing expenses or the fair rental value of his furnished house plus utilities. The church must designate annually the agreed-upon amount for the eligible pastor's housing allowance.

One of the biggest tax advantages for the pastor is for the church to, if at all possible, take his health, life, and disability insurance premiums out of his total compensation and make these an additional benefit. The church should do all it possibly can to financially protect the ministers who serve in the local congregation.

I believe the church should also be challenged to contribute an amount equal to a minimum of 10 percent of the pastor's income (within legal limits, of course) to a 403(b)(9) retirement vehicle as an employer contribution. I am aware of multitudes of churches who do this and many who do an additional "matching contribution" of 5 percent on top of this.

Another very practical way to enhance the pastor's financial security is for the church to provide additional income to their ministers equal to half of their SECA taxes. Remember that for Social Security purposes, ministers are self-employed and those SECA taxes exceed 15 percent. (Incidentally, and parenthetically, I would caution the pastor who seeks to opt out of Social Security. Few of us have the real discipline to seek to provide these protection benefits through private vehicles. There are also the issues of Medicare, potential disabilities, and the like that may not be wise to ignore. Seek wise counsel at this point.) Most ministers have a dual tax status. This means that although pastors are considered self-employed for Social Security purposes, they are usually employees for income tax purposes. This additional income can help offset the disadvantage this may place on the pastor or ministerial staff.

All this simply goes to say that the "laborer is worthy of his wages" (Luke 10:7), and it is the church's sacred duty and responsibility to "share in all good things with him who teaches" (Gal. 6:6).

PressurePoints

Perhaps the greatest plague of many modern ministers is found in the issue of debt and the pressure it brings to the pastor. It hangs like a dark and ominous cloud over the heads of many in ministry. The pastor should do all in his power to avoid it. Even though I've mentioned this in chapter 19, "The Pastor and His Possessions," it is important to enlarge on this subject here.

When my wife and I were married, we moved into a little house that was situated behind a larger house. It was less than five hundred square feet and consisted of a kitchen, a bedroom, and a bathroom. We used to laugh when she would bake a cake, because the floor slanted a good twelve to eighteen inches from one end of the house to the other, and her cakes would come out of the oven lopsided in the pan! In those days of early married life and ministry, we lived from week to week. We would most often arrive at the end of our money a few days before our next paycheck. However, we did something those first two years of marriage that we have never regretted. We did not go into debt for anything. If we could not afford it, we didn't get it. We did not even use a credit card for those first two years. It got us off to a disciplined and determined start in marriage. I am thankful to be able to say that over these decades of married life, we have never been in debt (with the exception of an asset like our home or an occasional car that always had an equity value more than our indebtedness), and we have never allowed a credit card charge to linger more than the thirty-day limit without paying it off in full. This took an unusual amount of sacrifice in the early years but has been a discipline that I recommend to every young pastor.

If you find yourself under the pressure of what seems to feel like the quicksand of debt, there are some important steps you should begin to take. First, admit it. This may seem somewhat obvious, but, unfortunately, it is not. Too many continue on as if it will somehow miraculously go away and thus live in continuous denial. Admitting it is the first step in any kind of repentance. Change your mind about your debt deception and admit you have a problem.

The next step is to stop it. Practice self-restraint and self-discipline. Quit watching the shopping networks on television where impulse buying is always at a premium. Resist the use of your credit cards. Perform some "plastic surgery" on yourself and cut most of them up and discontinue them. Admit it and then stop it.

Next, be honest with your creditors. Go to those you owe and assure them that you have every intention to pay the debt you owe them. Seek to work out a feasible and responsible repayment plan. Be honest about it. The worst thing you can do is ignore the issue. This can be a wonderful opportunity of testimony unto the Lord.

Then, once you have admitted it, stopped it, and been honest to those whom you owe, get some professional help from a trusted financial advisor on the subject. It may be in your best interest to seek a consolidation loan that would pay off all your creditors and leave you with only one payment each month. Be cautious at this point and seek trusted and guarded advice from someone you know you can trust.

Finally, go forward with a renewed commitment not to allow yourself to return to such a precarious situation. Have a disciplined plan and stay with it until your bills are paid off. Then begin to implement a strategy that will enable you to begin saving money instead of getting in debt.

Now, a final word about the pastor and his pay. There are few places where the pastor feels more pressure than at the point of his own need for adequate compensation. He trusts the Lord to meet all his needs and is confident that the Lord will do so. At the same time, he feels the pressure to provide for his wife and children and also to be able to protect them in the event of some unforeseen difficulty. The pressure usually comes in knowing with whom to talk related to the issue of compensation. He feels, and fears, that if he broaches the subject with church leadership, he will be construed as either unappreciative or greedy. Many pastors serve in places where lay leadership do not intentionally fail to meet his financial needs and obligations, but they simply do not give it thought for whatever reason. Who then will speak for the pastor? Many pastors are in need of an advocate at this point.

PulpitPoints

The pastor is worthy of his wages.

Luke 10:7

It may be that the pastorate is the most underpaid profession one can find. Many pastors are better educated and more adequately trained than many other professionals, and yet, for some reason, some churches do not do what is honorable in their compensation. There is a biblical basis for taking care of the pastor, and it is a stewardship and responsibility of every local, New Testament church today just as it was in first-generation Christianity.

- **The pastor's compensation should be purposely applied.**

  Jesus said, "The laborer is worthy of his wages" (Luke 10:7). The church should set out on purpose to adequately support the pastor with his finances. In fact, Scripture teaches the laborer in Christ's vineyard is really worthy of double compensation, and such appreciation should be intentionally expressed to him (1 Tim. 5:17). He should never be taken advantage of. The Lord has ordained that "those who preach the gospel should live from the gospel" (1 Cor. 9:14). To the Galatian church Paul put it like this: "Let him who is taught the word

share in all good things with him who teaches"
(Gal. 6:6).

- **The pastor's compensation should be personally accepted.**

  The pastor should not apologize or feel self-conscious about the compensation provided for him by his church. He should not shun it, nor should he be embarrassed to receive it. He is worthy of his wages, and there are adequate biblical mandates (several mentioned above) that justify it in the eyes of God and man.

- **The pastor's compensation should be properly appropriated.**

  I do not know many, if any, pastors who seek their compensation from their churches in order to provide a life of luxury for themselves. Most pastors I know hold loosely to the things of this world and properly appropriate their compensation to the Lord to meet the needs of their own families for whom they have biblical admonitions and to reach out to others who are in need.

The pastor and his pay is a peculiar subject for some churches, but it is one that needs to be addressed because "the laborer is worthy of his wages."

PersonalPoints

PersonalPoints

_____

_____

_____

_____

_____

_____

_____

_____

_____

_____

_____

_____

_____

_____

_____

_____

_____

_____

_____

PersonalPoints

25

The Pastor and His Pension

PowerPoints

The book of Proverbs is filled with hundreds of nuggets of common sense truth, many of which are encased in metaphors. Solomon was focused on the pastor's retirement years when he challenged us to "go to the ant, you sluggard! Consider her ways and be wise, which, having no captain, overseer or ruler, provides her supplies in the summer, and gathers her food in the harvest" (Prov. 6:6–8). Here, the wisest man who ever lived tells us we will be wise if we, like the ant, make preparation for the coming winter season of life. Unfortunately, many pastors give little thought or attention to this matter, somehow forgetting that God honors preparation and planning on our part as we trust him to ultimately meet our needs in this life.

Let me hasten to say that retirement should most likely never be a large part of the pastor's thinking process. Who of us ever intends to retire from ministry and the service of the Lord Jesus? I am speaking here of vocational retirement from our church or place of service and not ministry retirement. Retirement planning is a three-legged stool. One leg of the stool is the provision that will one day come our way through Social Security benefits. The second leg is that which you will one day receive from your 403(b) or other retirement vehicle. The final leg to a successful retirement is the leg of your personal savings. The wise pastor realizes that all three legs are not only important but imperative if he is to live with any semblance of financial security and dignity in his declining years.

Most financial planners suggest that a retirement income goal should equal at least 70–80 percent of your pre-retirement income. This means it is imperative that the pastor begin early on in his career to "go to the ant and be wise" by laying aside a figure monthly for his later years. There is an important principle called compound interest, which is virtually mandatory if you expect your savings and retirement to grow significantly across the years. This important principle will be discussed below under both our "PracticalPoints" and "PressurePoints."

PracticalPoints

In my position at GuideStone Financial Resources, dealing with thousands of pastors and their retirement needs, I find that this is a subject that many pastors never give much thought to until they are reaching vocational retirement, and it is almost too late. Most pastors I know are underpaid and overworked and spend long hours in pastoral ministry and simply do not think they have the money or time to think or do anything about this important issue.

Practically speaking, retirement planning is like running a marathon. It is not a sprint like a one hundred-meter dash. It is not a middle-distance event like the eight hundred meters or the mile run. It is not a field event like the long jump or the high jump. It is a marathon. Effective and successful marathon runners know there are four stages to the race. You must get off to a good start, you must set a constant pace, you must pick up the pace near the end, and you must sprint the last few yards to the finish line.

The first important thing in running a marathon is to get off to a good start. If you get too far behind the crowd in the beginning, you will have to spend a lot of energy breaking through the mass of men and women ahead of you in order to be able to set your pace later. Retirement planning is the same way. It demands that we get started right and that means early on in our ministry. The wise seminary student and first-time pastor sees this importance. For example, a thirty-year-old pastor may only need to contribute an amount equal to 6 percent of his pay to receive a retirement benefit equal to 50 percent of his final annual salary at age sixty-five. However, if the same pastor waited just ten years to begin contributing to his retirement vehicle, he would need to contribute 11 percent of his pay until he was sixty-five in order to receive the same 50 percent goal. This illustrates the principle of compound interest and also the necessity of a good start to retirement planning.

The next stage of the marathon is the stage in which the runner sets a consistent pace. Here he finds his zone, and the greater part of the miles of the race are spent here. He sets a pace, gets in his groove, and runs this way for miles and miles. The same is true with our retirement planning. Once we have determined our risk tolerance and time horizon, we factor in our asset allocation and set our pace for years, trusting it to work for us. Like the marathon runner, there will be hills and valleys on the financial landscape, but once the pastor has determined the necessary factors above, he sets his pace and devotes his energies and efforts to the ministry to which God calls him.

The third stage in marathon running is when we get near the end of the race. After getting off to a good start and running the long distance at our set pace, we pick it up when we get near the end. This phase of the race is called the "kick." And so it is with our own retirement planning. Once our children are grown and gone and there is disposable income, we begin to maximize our retirement contribution. Here we kick in additional monies in order to take advantage of tax savings and in some cases deferred compensation.

Finally, we come to the end, the finish line. And right before we get there, we give it all we have. We sprint toward the tape. We seek to finish strong so that we do not simply stumble and fall over the line. For the pastor whom God calls to ministry, finishing strong is vitally important to our gospel witness. The pastor who has gotten a good start in his retirement preparation, maintained a constant pace of contributions across the years, and has maximized his efforts in his latter years can sprint across the finish line knowing he has wisely obtained some measure of financial security and will be able to volunteer on mission whenever and wherever God may lead him as he retools for ministry in retirement.

PressurePoints

There is a tremendous amount of pressure upon the pastor as he realistically seeks to provide for his declining years. The three-legged stool mentioned above has some wobbly legs for the modern pastor. For one thing, Social Security has some potential uncertainties about it in the future. The leg of savings is not wobbly; it is almost broken. The average savings rate for all Americans today is less than 1 percent annually. Many pastors have a difficult time living from week to week, much less being able to save any substantial amount of money. This leaves the leg of our retirement vehicle. There are many advantages to being with an organization like GuideStone.

Another challenge is the clarion call to get started early in your ministry. Let me give you a revealing statistic. If, at age thirty-five, a pastor begins to contribute $50 per month to his retirement and does so until he is sixty-five, he could potentially accumulate a balance of $70,881. (This is simply illustrative and assumes an 8 percent annual return.) But note what happens if he starts a little earlier. This same pastor starting at age twenty-five, instead of thirty-five, contributing the same $50 per month, would have a nest egg of $162,090 at age sixty-five. If he contributed $100 each month, he would have $141,761 if he began at age thirty-five and $324,180 if he got started a little earlier at age twenty-five! This is the value of having your money working for you, which we call compound interest.

Pastor, the point is simple. Get started! No matter what your age, get started in this race. It is never too late for a new beginning. This is a sacred stewardship and one that should be a priority on any pastor's list of wise things to accomplish.

PulpitPoints

Retired or retooled?

Proverbs 6:6–8

The pastor is marching through life toward that place of vocational retirement. There is a tragic epidemic among thousands of retired pastors. They are not ready for it financially. I am sad to say that thousands of pastors in their retirement and declining years are living on $200 a month or less in retirement benefits. Most of them pastored out at the crossroads in the small churches and were never able to make financial preparation. However, some of them find themselves in this predicament because when they were able to do something about it in their earlier years, they did little, and in some sad cases, nothing. While there are relief ministries to help meet their needs, there is a better way.

Solomon offers some wise counsel to pastors today in Proverbs 6. He calls upon those of us he refers to as "sluggards" and challenges us to go and observe the ant. He says we should consider the ways of the ant and be wise, for the ant stores up food in summer so that when winter comes there will be an adequate supply. If that is good advice for an ant, that is also good advice for a preacher of the gospel!

- **A problem with retirement preparation**

    Solomon refers to those who procrastinate as "sluggards." The word refers to laziness, but even more than that it refers to procrastination on the part of certain people. Here is the man who knows what to do and puts it off. This is the problem with retirement preparation on the part of many pastors. They simply think it is an issue that they will think about in a few years and keep putting it off throughout their lifetimes.

- **A picture of retirement preparation**

Solomon suggests we go to the ant and study its ways and in so doing, become wise. He paints a picture of the ant in these verses. The ant has no leader, no commander that is directing and giving orders about what to do or where to go or how to get there. The ant has no overseer to inspect his work and see that it is done properly. He has no ruler to push him and prod him to achievement. And yet the ant works better than most pastors. The ant works with the future in mind.

- **A possibility of retirement preparation**

Solomon says wisdom comes in observing this obvious object lesson. The ant doesn't simply live for the current moment but lives in anticipation of its future needs. The ants store and gather their food in summer while it is warm and long before the winter comes upon them. Yes, pastor, "go to the ant and be wise" as it relates to your own retirement preparation. You may feel the warmth of summer now, but winter is coming.

Can you imagine what could happen if we could get the next couple of generations of pastors to "go to the ant and be wise" and begin preparing systematically for their retirement? These next generations are going to live longer than any generations in modern history. Many of our retired pastors will have twenty or more active and healthy years of life and potential service after they vocationally retire from local church ministry. If we can help them get to that place of vocational retirement with financial security and dignity, we will be able to help unleash upon this world the greatest force of volunteers on mission the world has ever witnessed. And the latter years of our lives and ministries can become our most productive ever. Pastor, don't think about "retiring." Go to the "ant and be wise" and think about "retooling." God is not through with you yet.

PersonalPoints

PersonalPoints

PersonalPoints

26

The Pastor and His Prize

PowerPoints

The faithful pastor has a special prize awaiting him. It is referred to as the "pastor's crown." This is the reward especially reserved for him and spoken of by Peter in his first epistle, "And when the Chief Shepherd appears, you will receive the crown of glory that does not fade away" (1 Peter 5:4). At his glorious appearing, God will set the faithful pastor apart from everyone else for an unusual recognition and reward. Think of it, pastor, the Lord himself will look at you and say, "Well done, good and faithful servant," and he will place upon your head the "crown of glory." All those times of being unappreciated or misunderstood will pale into nothingness on that glorious day. It will be worth it all.

I watched W. A. Criswell die ... for days and weeks and months. He lived out his last days in the home of his friend and partner in ministry, Jack Pogue. Dr. Criswell lay for those months in a hospital bed in Mr. Pogue's den with the faithful layman sleeping nightly on the floor meeting his frequent needs. In those last days the great preacher-pastor, medicated and dying of cancer, would often wake up his friend in the middle of the night preaching the gospel. He would be speaking of his glorious appearing and would often tell Jack to make sure the counselors were ready as there were going to be many responding to the invitation to accept Christ. What that old warrior-saint had stored in his heart and mind for a lifetime of ministry now burst forth even in his sedated moments. People who would come to visit were often asked, "Oh, have you come for the revival?" The last time I was with him when he was conscious (the day before he died), I read to him of the Lord's coming, the marriage of the Lamb, the judgment seat of Christ, and the crown of glory. As he lay there, a smile came across his face. He had lived his life looking for our "blessed hope, His glorious appearing." And now, he died in anticipation of that day.

The faithful pastor has a prize awaiting him. It is one that will never fade away. What a hope for the pastor who now endures all sorts of trials and testings. It will be worth it all when we see Jesus.

PracticalPoints

Paul's hope for every pastor is wrapped up in the words of 2 Timothy 4:1–5. These words carry not only the hope of every pastor but also the imperative that we be found faithful in our calling. James reminds us that those of us who teach are judged by higher standings than others (James 3:1). The pastor must be ever mindful that his ministry takes place under the watchful eye of the Judge himself. This is not like an earthly judge who hears the facts and considers the merits of the case. This Judge knows all the facts and his eyes "run to and fro throughout the whole earth, to show Himself strong on behalf of those whose hearts are fixed on Him" (2 Chron. 16:9). The pastor must realize the seriousness of his calling and local church assignment and be dedicated to it without reservation. The perfect Judge is watching and will render His judgment on the nature, faithfulness, and motives of the pastor's efforts. Being daily mindful of whom we will one day stand before should keep our priorities in line and keep us focused on our calling.

As a young preacher, my pastor, W. Fred Swank, spoke to me often about the seriousness of my calling and the issue of the pastor's prize. He lived in the fear of God. And Dr. Swank taught me, as mentioned before, that walking in the fear of the Lord was not the fear that the Lord was going to put his hand of retribution upon me if I did something wrong or said something indifferent. For him, it was the attitude of walking in the fear that God might take his hand off of him, remove his blessing and/or his anointing from him. That is it! The pastor should go about his life walking in the fear of the Lord. That is, the fear that God might take his hand of blessings and anointing off him. That attitude would make a difference in some things the pastor said, some places he might go, some things he might watch, and some things he might do. I believe this is what Paul was getting at when he said to the Corinthians that he feared that "once I have preached to others that I might become a castaway." In other words, Paul lived with this fear that God might put him on the shelf. As we fulfill our role and high calling as pastors, may we live each day in light of "that day" in such a way that we too will receive the "crown of glory that does not fade away."

PressurePoints

Lest the pastor should begin to feel a tinge of pride in that he is striving toward the "crown of glory," he should remember what each of us will do with the various crowns that are mentioned in Scripture. We will take them to the throne of the Lord Jesus and lay them at his precious feet. All glory and honor will be only his in "that day." The motivation for the pastor should never be in receiving some crown but in daily giving Christ all the glory. We will one day "cast all our crowns at Jesus's feet."

There seems to be two distinct pressures that come upon the pastor at the point of our Lord's return. There are some pastors who seem to be so caught up in the second coming of our Lord that they often forget to appropriate all that his first coming means to us. I am speaking here of what Paul said in Colossians 1:27, "Christ in you, the hope of glory." Matters of eschatology and prophecy have a way of capturing the allure and attention of many in such a way that they become overly consuming, and the pastor gets out of balance. While I am looking for the Savior, I am still about the business of seeking, with the help of the Holy Spirit, to appropriate all that his first coming avails to me.

The other pressure comes in being so consumed in ministry from a relational and strategic standpoint that matters of future events are not a concern and are seldom mentioned. I believe we are pastoring today in a time when this is more an issue than an overt emphasis on the Second Coming. Some pastors today speak nothing of the return of the Lord, of coming judgments, or of rewards for the faithful followers of Christ. No wonder so many live without hope. Christ is the personification of our hope. He is our "blessed hope" in his glorious appearing. The early church lived daily with a word on their lips. The word was "Maranatha!" It means "the Lord is coming!" Church members greeted one another with that word. They saluted one another with that word. They said their good-byes to one another with that word. They shouted it to one another above the fires of their own martyrdom. They lived in anticipation of the Lord's coming. The wise pastor today will lead his people to remember there is a day appointed on God's calendar when Christ will come to judge the world in righteousness.

The pastor is awaiting a blessed event. "When the Chief Shepherd appears, you will receive the crown of glory that does not fade away" (1 Peter 5:4). Pastor, be faithful and live in constant anticipation of "that day."

PulpitPoints

The prize before us

James 5:7–12

"Be patient … until the coming of the Lord" (James 5:7). These words of admonition should be heeded by the faithful servant of Christ as he awaits his reward. The Lord's promise to every pastor is that when "the Chief Shepherd appears, you will receive the crown of glory that does not fade away" (1 Peter 5:4).

There are always events on the horizon that point to the fact that these could well be the days that could usher in "His glorious appearing." The Bible does, in fact, signal several conditions that will be prevalent when the Lord returns. We are told to be watching for a polluted pulpit (2 Tim. 4:2–4), a particular place (Amos 9:14–15), a peculiar people (Deut. 28:37–65; Ezek. 36:24), a powerful politic (Dan. 7:15–25), a popular politician (1 John 2:18), and a pluralistic philosophy of new age thought that will seek to unite the world under one banner.

What should be the Christian's response as we all await the coming of our Lord? It is the same as it was in the early church. James, the godly leader of the Jerusalem church, left us a word not only for his day but also for ours. Inspired not by world events, but by the Holy Spirit himself, James tells us what we should be doing until the Lord comes and bestows gifts upon the redeemed, which, I might remind us, will then, in turn, be laid at the Lord's precious feet.

- **Look upward ... be calm (v. 7).**

- **Look inward ... be clean (vv. 8–9).**

- **Look backward ... be challenged (vv. 10–11).**

- **Look forward ... be consistent (v. 12).**

Yes, be patient until the Lord's coming. These should be days for the pastor and his people to be looking up, but also looking in, looking back, and looking forward. Pastor, "when the Chief Shepherd appears, you will receive the crown of glory that does not fade away."

PersonalPoints

PersonalPoints

_____

_____

_____

_____

_____

_____

_____

_____

_____

_____

_____

_____

_____

_____

_____

_____

_____

PersonalPoints

_____

_____

_____

_____

_____

_____

_____

_____

_____

_____

_____

_____

_____

_____

_____

_____

_____

_____

Appendix A

GuideStone Financial Resources has been meeting the retirement needs of pastors since 1918. At GuideStone our task and calling is primarily to provide a retirement vehicle for those in ministry. We have a simple vision statement that defines what we do. Our vision statement says that we exist "to honor the Lord by being a lifelong partner with our participants in enhancing their financial security." It is our job to seek to help pastors reach the time of vocational retirement with enough financial security that they can live in dignity. The next couple of generations are going to have as many as twenty or twenty-five good and healthy years after their vocational retirement. If we can fulfill our calling, then we will be able to unleash on the world the greatest force of volunteers on mission the world has ever seen. And we can help make those last years of life the most productive for many of our participants. In our vision statement, we find our motivation. We exist to "honor the Lord." This is what motivates us. If we honor him in what we do, we will be well on our way to serving our participants. We also find our message in our vision statement. It is to be a "lifelong partner with our participants." We don't want them to simply think of us when they need to retire but all along the way. Finally, we find our mandate as well. It is to "enhance their financial security." Our vision defines our task and is the lens through which we view our work daily. Vision is vital.

GuideStone makes available a booklet titled, *Planning Financial Support*, which is free for the asking. This workbook offers practical help and provides sample policies and forms the church can use to be a wise steward of its pastor's financial needs. Our Southern Baptist pastors who are in our program receive absolutely free a survivor's benefit of up to $100,000 and a disability program that provides $500 monthly in the event of disability regardless of the amount of their accounts. This is a safety net that every church should be providing for their pastor.

Also, we at GuideStone will be happy to write a letter to your lay leadership and enclose our Planning Financial Support workbook, which can guide them as to how to best structure the compensation package and challenge them to do the right thing for their pastor. Upon request, we can also provide up-to-date information on confidential salary surveys by respective church sizes and locales. Simply visit our Web site at www.GuideStone .org; write us at GuideStone Financial Resources, 2401 Cedar Springs Road, Dallas, TX 75201; or call toll-free at 1-888-98-GUIDE (1-888-984-8433).

Scripture Index

About the Author

For more than twenty-five years, O. S. Hawkins served pastorates including the First Baptist Church in Fort Lauderdale, Florida, and the First Baptist Church in Dallas, Texas. A native of Fort Worth, he has three earned degrees (BBA, MDiv, and DMin) and several honorary degrees. He is president of GuideStone Financial Resources, which serves two hundred thousand pastors, church staff members, missionaries, doctors, nurses, university professors, and other workers of various Christian organizations with their retirement and benefit service needs. He is the author of more than twenty-five books and preaches regularly at Bible conferences, evangelism conferences, and churches across the nation. He and his wife, Susie, have two married daughters and six grandchildren.

CPSIA information can be obtained
at www.ICGtesting.com
Printed in the USA
LVHW050110210122
708906LV00007B/11